Ramy Nima

The wrath of Allah

Islamic revolution and reaction in Iran

Pluto  Press

London and Sydney

First published in 1983 by
Pluto Press Limited,
The Works, 105a Torriano Avenue,
London NW5 2RX
and Pluto Press Australia Limited,
P.O. Box 199, Leichhardt, New South Wales
2040, Australia

Photoset and printed in Great Britain by
Photobooks (Bristol) Ltd
Bound by W. H. Ware and Sons Limited,
Tweed Road, Clevedon, Avon

Map on page 131 by Swanston Graphics, Derby

British Library Cataloguing in Publication Data
Nima, Ramy
   The wrath of Allah.
   1. Islam and politics – Iran
   2. Revolutionists – Iran   3. Iran – Politics
   and governments – 1979–
   I. Title
   322.4'2'0955   D5318.8

ISBN 0-86104-733-8

Contents

Part three: Islamic order, reaction and war

Preface

This book is a descriptive account of the political revolution that transformed the Pahlavi dictatorship into an Islamic theocratic order. It is divided into three parts, starting with a brief résumé of the background to the social, economic and political development of modern Iran. The second part traces the mass struggle against the dictatorship from the days of protest in 1977 to the revolutionary uprising of 1979. Part three covers the process by which the clergy achieved its dominance, the formation of the Islamic order and the Iran–Iraq war.

I am grateful to many people for their help in the writing of this book. Here I will only mention those to whom I owe a special debt. First and foremost my special thanks are due to Azin Bazini for his scrupulous reading and criticism of the entire manuscript, his valuable comments and suggestions. Also to be thanked are Azar-Barzin Mehr for his much appreciated comments on Islam and Shi'ism; Nasir Pakdaman for his reading of the first draft of Part One; my parents for providing me with much detailed information and encouragement; Frankie, who was the first to carefully read the entire work and whose suggestions were of enormous value; and Mrs E. H. for typing the manuscript with great speed and accuracy.

I would like also to thank Mike Kidron, who first proposed to me that I write this study and who encouraged me at a moment when I needed reassurance; and many thanks are due to Elana Dallas for her editing which greatly improved the original.

Finally, it only remains to say that I am solely responsible if there are any errors of judgement or fact.

Part one:

The background

1. Foreign domination

It was during the second half of the nineteenth century that Britain and Tsarist Russia stepped up their level of influence and intervention in Iranian affairs. For nearly a century the Iranian state had been haunted by the interventionist power of Russia. Britain had, by 1850, fully recognised the strategic importance of Iran as a gateway to India. To safeguard its interests in India, Britain could not allow Russia mastery over Iran. At the same time the Russians were clearly reluctant to expose their southern borders to British military, political and economic penetration. It was principally this imperialist rivalry between Russia and Britain which prevented the colonisation of Iran by either power, as one could not advance militarily without risking war with the other. The non-colonial form of the domination of Iran stems from this regional power struggle between the two imperial states.

Both Russia and Britain had a vested interest in ensuring that the organisation and structure of the Iranian state remained weak, as well as in the continuation of a corrupt dynasty – the Qajars – at its head. Generally in colonised countries a strong state was established within a relatively short time. However, in the case of Iran governmental reforms and modernisation of the administration and military organisations were conspicuously absent. This form of political domination, which involved intrigues, interventions and the manipulation of Iran's political affairs, affected the economic life of the country, and therefore the development of its class structure and the relations between the classes. For the Iranian state, despite its weakness and disunity among the ruling class (that is, the royal family, the high echelons of the state, tribal chiefs, senior religious officials and the landed aristocracy) was significant not only politically but also economically. It was the biggest landowner, controlled access to the main economic resources of the country, and had power over taxes, duties, customs and trade routes. The power of the state in the mid-nineteenth century was far less than it had been in the sixteenth and seventeenth centuries. Nevertheless, it penetrated every aspect of life and was always, to a greater or lesser extent, involved in the economy.

Foreign economic penetration

The commercial and economic penetration of Iran by foreign interests grew in importance from the middle of the nineteenth century. Although both Russia and Britain made significant inroads into Iranian trade and commercial activities, Britain – then the most advanced capitalist country in the world – had far greater success in dominating Iranian trade, at least up to the 1880s.

However, British investment in Iran was relatively low in the nineteenth century. Capital investment in, for example, raw material production in Iran was extremely small compared to that in the British colonies proper.[1] Foreign investment in Iran, at least before the advent of the oil industry, was far less significant than foreign imports of manufactured commodities. For example, large quantities of textiles were imported from Europe, in particular from Britain, with disastrous consequences for the Iranian handicraft industry.

The commercial rivalry between Britain and Russia became more intense from about 1870, with competition for concessions feeding the corruption of the Iranian ruling class and extending the grip of foreign interests over Iran's economy. The most famous was the Reuter concession of 1872. Baron de Reuter was granted a concession which gave him a comprehensive monopoly of mining, banking, railway construction, and the development of all future irrigation works, roads, the telegraph system and industrial factories. All this for a payment of £40,000 and a percentage of the profits from the customs duties.[2]

The Russians received concessions on a number of projects from road construction to monopolies over the fishing industry in the Caspian sea, and over the insurance of transport in the north of Iran. The British were never far behind. One of the most important concessions (in terms of its social and political effects) was the 1890 tobacco concession granted to a British company which awarded it a monopoly of the production, sale and export of tobacco, in return for a gift of £25,000, an annual rent of £15,000 to the state, plus 25 per cent of the profits. The concession granted a 50-year monopoly over the production, sale and export of tobacco.[3] Iranian merchants would have no right to export tobacco (a very profitable trade at the time) and they would lose their position as 'middlemen' in Iran itself. The concession also affected traders and merchants who would have to purchase tobacco at the company's prices. In April 1981 the small traders that were going to be affected by the tobacco concession (mainly in the bazaars) went on strike and shut down their businesses, first in Shiraz (a major tobacco producing area) and then in all the major towns and cities. There was, in effect, a general strike of merchants, shopkeepers and traders. The close connection between the clergy and the bazaar and the clergy's financial dependence on merchants and traders – together with its opposition to foreign influence on the religious and traditional way of life – meant that it was not long before the religious authorities gave their support to the strike. They called for a boycott of the use of tobacco by all Moslems. The extent of discontent, with bazaar strikes and demonstrations on the streets of Tehran (as well as Russian hostility to the tobacco concession) combined to force the state to annul the concession.

Oil

In 1901, a concession was granted to a British engineer, William D'Arcy, which guaranteed exclusive rights to exploit all aspects of petroleum production. For this the Iranian state was to receive 16 per cent of the profits and was promised a cash payment of £20,000 plus £20,000 in shares. In fact the cash payment was never made. In 1908 oil was found in commercially viable quantities and on 14 April 1909 the Anglo-Persian Oil Company (APOC) was formed with a share capital of £2 million. The Iranian, or rather British, oil industry had come into being. By 1912 a refinery in Abadan, in the southern tip of south-western Iran, had been built. For many years oil production was exclusively geared for export. Iran, whose demand for oil was extremely limited, imported it from Russia.

The export of oil required efficient contact between the point of production and markets abroad. British investment concentrated on providing facilities and transportation (pipelines, ports, shipping, etc.) for the oil industry. The investment policies of APOC neglected completely the development of infrastructural facilities considered unnecessary for oil production and export.

Profits were immense in relation to the amount invested by APOC. Original APOC investment in Iran amounted to £21,656,252, of which the British government contributed some £5 million. In return, the shareholders of APOC received £115 million, with a further £400 to £500 million being re-invested in the industry. In addition, £175 million went to the British state in taxation. At a conservative estimate this modest investment of some £22 million produced for British capital something like £700 to £800 million in its 50-odd years of operation. That is an average of £16 million a year. The Iranian state, in the same period, received a mere £105 million.[4] There were further losses by exempting oil exports from customs duties and export taxes. The lost customs duties, cost some £6 million a year. The export taxes would have amounted to £19 million and £20 million in the years 1927 and 1935, for which they have been calculated.

Nearly all the towns in the oil area of southern Iran either came into being entirely for the benefit of the APOC, or depended to a great extent on its activities. In effect the whole of the area could be considered an APOC 'colony'. Outside the limits of company-owned property, there was stagnation and decay caused by the increase in population without a corresponding increase in amenities. Of all the wealth appropriated by the company a mere trickle went to improve the conditions of its workers. The attitude of the company was typically colonialist; almost complete racial segregation in all matters from employment and accommodation to company transport services.[5] Types of accommodation, for example, were classified into three grades but most Iranian workers fell outside this classification and had to fend for themselves. In 1949, 80 per cent of directly employed wage-workers were not provided with housing by the company. There were an additional 16,000 labourers working for the company's contractors, who lived as best they could in shanty towns. No adequate health care was provided by the company for its workforce, while the British managerial and technical staff had their own hospital facilities.[6]

Until 1946 the minimum wage for an unskilled worker remained constant at 4 rials, or one shilling, a day. In 1946, when the cost of living had risen by more than 900 per cent, the minimum wage became 14 rials. Even when the Iranian government raised this to 40 rials, it was merely bringing its purchasing power back to the 1936 level. The wage was calculated to secure only the barest necessities of existence for a single man.[7]

Out of a total of 42,614 direct employees on daily wage rates in 1949, only 1,167 received as little as the minimum wage of 40 rials per day. However, 40,348, or about 95 per cent, received less than 80 rials a day, or double the bare minimum. By comparison, US oil workers received at that time $1.65 (137 rials) *an hour*.[8]

APOC labour relations were dismal and the company dealt ruthlessly with strikes and other disputes, using its own police force. In 1922 the Iranian workers, supported by most of the Indian white-collar and technical orkers, struck for a wage increase of 100 per cent. To quell the strike British troops were brought in; most of the organisers were arrested and about 2,000 Indian workers dismissed, although eventually a 75 per cent wage increase was granted. There were no major strikes after this until May 1929 when another industry-wide strike took place. The strike was put down, but this time by the Iranian authorities; 200 workers were imprisoned for two to three years and when released they were prohibited from returning to the company's domain. Five of the leading organisers were sent to Tehran prisons and released only after the Reza Shah's abdication in 1941. The relative 'freedom' during the war and post-war period allowed greater industrial and political activity among the oil workers. The deep grievances between the company management and its Iranian workers exploded once again in May 1946, when a general strike of oil workers was called. The Iranian government ordered in the troops and proclaimed martial law in the affected area. On 16 July 1946, as a result of this government action, another strike broke out in Abadan which involved an estimated 100,000 workers from nearly all major establishments in the area. The troops were ordered to fire on the demonstrating strikers and, according to one conservative estimate, 17 workers were killed and about 150 wounded.[9]

This was, in a sense, a dress rehearsal for the struggle that was to follow over the nationalisation of the oil industry in which the oil workers (and the working class generally) played a very significant role. Strikes and demonstrations involving tens of thousands of workers took place in support of oil nationalisation. The demand for nationalisation by the oil workers was only part of the struggle against miserable social conditions, discriminatory management, the company's anti-union attitudes and actions in the past, and, of course, low wages.

2. Economic development

In the nineteenth and early twentieth centuries, the most important role of the state in the economy was its power to grant concessions to foreign companies. All these concessions benefited exclusively the foreign companies' home country and none – including that of oil – was intended to have, nor did have, any real or substantial influence on the development of the Iranian economy. The economic infrastructure remained primitive and the Iranian state itself was under great pressure as a result of internal conflicts and regional rebellions and external intervention. By mid-1911, the provinces were embroiled in tribal warfare and by the end of that year Russian and British troops moved into Iran. In the autumn of 1914, Ottoman contingents invaded the western regions, while German agents were arming the southern tribes against the British. From 1909 to 1921 the central government had no power outside the capital.

The intense competition between the advanced capitalist countries had, by the turn of the century, resulted in the increasing importance of two interrelated phenomena: first, the nation state as a dominant force within capitalism; and second, warfare and militarism as an essential element of the capitalist system.

This transformation had far-reaching consequences for the backward countries on the periphery of the system and for the relationship between them and the advanced countries of the centre. Iran, despite its extreme backwardness, was not unaffected. The First World War resulted in the occupation of its territory by Russia and Britain. The Bolshevik victory in 1917 and the changes that occurred as a result of the First World War, dramatically changed the pattern of imperialist activity in Iran. The revolution of 1917 meant the end of Russian imperialism and, although British troops left Iran at the end of the war, the threat of spreading Bolshevism forced a change in Britain's attitude to Iran.[1]

Britain saw a need for a strong state in Iran, one which would remain under British control.[2] The 1919 Anglo-Persian Agreement was an attempt to ensure this: it provided for British advisers (who had 'adequate powers') in principal ministries, and for British officers to organise the armed forces with the British Government providing equipment and munitions. After eighteen months the agreement was rejected. By 1920, tribal chiefs were in control over much of the southern and western regions and autonomous governments had been established in the two northern regions of Azarbaijan and Gilan. Growing internal strife, and separatist movements in control in many provinces, demanded the formation of a centralised state.[3] This need was eventually met by the coup d'état of 1921 which brought a Cossack officer, Reza Khan, into power.

From this point on can be seen a greater involvement of the state in stimulating capitalist development in the economy and a definite tendency towards state capitalism. However, the state never managed to take full control of production.

After the Iranian debt to the USSR was cancelled by the signing of a treaty in 1921, and subsequent increases in oil revenue, enough funds were available for the state to begin an industrial development programme, although during the reign of Reza Shah (1926–41) a great deal of emphasis was placed on expanding and modernising the military and bureaucratic apparatus instead. For example, nearly all the state oil revenues were spent on military equipment.

The state did establish certain protectionist measures to stimulate private domestic investment, and created a sizeable state capitalist sector. Apart from munitions, the heavily subsidised state monopolies were mostly established to promote the production of consumer goods such as tea and sugar.[4] By the end of the 1930s the state had established 64 factories and was allocating about 20 per cent of its budget to industrial development.[5] The number of employed industrial workers increased by 250 per cent between 1934 and 1938,[6] and by 1946, approximately 50 per cent of industrial workers employed in large-scale manufacturing industry (10 or more workers), were working in the state capitalist sector.

However, the agricultural sector, with a labour force of well over 3.5 million, had received hardly any state attention. The most important sector of all – oil – remained out of state control.

One important consequence was the programme of state capitalist investment. Another was the state's attempt to control foreign trade, which was regarded as essential to limit certain imports and reduce the demand for foreign exchange. This was a first attempt to establish a national policy to protect new home industries,[7] encourage production for export and, if possible, obtain better terms in the world market.[8]

It seemed that Iran was on its way to some degree of economic independence, but in practice this was far from the truth. Very few of the state's efforts to control foreign trade were effective.[9] Corruption, mismanagement and 'administrative and accounting inefficiencies' in the state sector meant that few of the newly established state-owned factories were profitable. The unreliable supply of domestically produced commodities, their inferior quality and relatively high cost kept the demand for imports as high as ever. Reza Shah's attempt at economic nationalism was a failure.

Meanwhile, in the international arena, vicious competition between the advanced capitalist nations resulted in the Second World War. In Iran, the state's increasing use of direct and open violence to control class and ethnic opposition, and Reza Shah's pro-German attitude, gave the British and Russians a good excuse to take direct military action. August 1941 saw an Anglo-Soviet invasion to safeguard oil installations, open a new corridor for Soviet aid and remove the threat of German intrigue. This brought to an end Reza Shah's attempt at economic nationalism. He went into exile, and his son became Shah – the second monarch of the Pahlavi dynasty. However, the state had been discredited by its failure to resist the invasion, and was threatened by opposition forces allowed new political freedom by the occupying armies. After 16 years of Reza Shah's repression, political organisations flourished, and in the provinces struggles by the national minorities led to autonomous governments in Azarbaijan and Kurdistan. In the cities, unrest by the Tudeh (Communist) Party threatened the social order. It was not until 1947 that the Shah, with the aid of US military assistance and the USSR's abandonment of Azarbaijan and Kurdistan, finally regained control of the whole country.

The post-war period

The period of post-war recovery saw the inauguration of the First Plan (1949–56) which was intended to be a 'big push' towards economic development and self-sufficiency. In practice, however, its achievements fell far short of its aims. The state managed to establish only six new industrial plants, to construct some road and rail networks, and to carry out a few minor developments in the agricultural sector.[10] The 'big push' to achieve self-sufficiency in fact turned out to be 'a feeble puff'.[11]

The principal difficulty seemed to be – at least to most of the protagonists of economic nationalism in Iran – the total foreign control of the country's most important resource, namely oil. The major portion of the surplus generated by it never reached the state's coffers; only 15 per cent of state revenue was derived from the oil concession in the south. Yet the oil industry was a potentially crucial sector and, moreover, a clearly visible symbol of economic domination.[12]

From 1946 onwards, nationalist feeling in Iran was directed against the continued ownership of Iran's oil by the Anglo-Iranian Oil Company, formerly the Anglo-Persian Oil Company. (Its name had been changed in the 1930s.) The oil protest movement gained widespread support among the urban population and amongst the oil workers themselves. Popular sentiment and demonstrations, as well as the strike by oil workers in the Anglo-Iranian Oil Company fields in 1951, forced even some conservative members of parliament to approve the Oil Nationalisation Act of parliamentary deputy Mohammad Mossadeq. Mossadeq's popularity had turned the majority of deputies in the *majlis* (parliament) to a pro-Mossadeq position and they elected him as Prime Minister in May 1951. Heading a loose coalition organisation called the National Front, his first move as premier was to deal with the oil issue. In the early summer of 1951, he sent a committee to Khuzistan to take control of the oil installations, and negotiations with the Anglo-Iranian Oil Company broke off. In June 1951, the oil industry was nationalised. The state-owned company, National Iranian Oil Company (NIOC) took over all the fixed assets of the Anglo-Iranian Oil Company. There was an almost immediate boycott of Iranian oil by all the major international oil companies, causing the production and marketing of crude oil and refined products to come to a virtual standstill. Oil production fell from 243 million barrels in 1950 to around 8 million in 1952–53.[13] 'Each of the seven sisters [as the oil giants were known] had an interest in proving to the Iranians and to other potential miscreants that they could quite well do without their oil.'[14]

The boycott failed to produce either a change of attitude or a change of Mossadeq's government. Despite the boycott, Mossadeq's nationalist government was quite successful in managing the economy and Iran accumulated a trade surplus on its non-oil trade account. There was some improvement in agricultural production and the government was able to export certain agricultural products. However, the government's efforts could not possibly succeed in the long run without a settlement of the oil dispute.

Both the British and US governments were extremely concerned about the possibility of a communist takeover and Russian advances into Iran, especially since the Tudeh Party was growing at a tremendous rate. From their point of view drastic action had to be taken to 'save' Iran – and, of course, Iranian oil – from the hands of the communists. In 1953, a CIA coup, with the help of British Intelligence, finally restored 'order'. The coup toppled Mossadeq and by reinstating the dictatorial powers of the Shah established a new 'friendly' regime.

By this time it had become obvious that the Anglo-Iranian Oil Company (now renamed British Petroleum) could no longer have a monopoly of Iranian oil. In 1954 a consortium was established which included the 'seven sisters' and France's Compagnie Française des Pétroles, plus a number of independent oil companies. Formally, the National Iranian Oil Company remained the owner of the oil fields and the refinery, and the consortium bought oil from it. In practice, because of their control over the world market, the members of the consortium were the real masters of oil production in Iran. Nor did the Iranian state receive any additional revenue on oil industry assets which it owned but which were being used by the consortium. However the nationalisation struggle had forced certain improvements. The profit-sharing arrangement was amended to give the Iranian state 50 per cent, compared to 16 per cent received previously. In 1974, a 'participants agreement' which had been kept secret from the Iranian government was revealed. Under this agreement, signed by the eight giant companies of the consortium, a formula ('aggregate programmed quantity') had been established which in effect controlled the amount of revenue the Iranian state would receive.[15]

If nationalisation of the oil industry had symbolised the struggle for economic independence and freedom from the constraints of the world market dominated by international capital, the establishment of the consortium shattered that illusion.

Economic development under the Shah

The dream of economic independence was shattered with the 1953 coup and the nightmare of military dictatorship became, once more, a reality. But the defeat of economic nationalism did not mean the end of state capitalist development.

It was from this period on that, as a result of state intervention, Iranian industry began its slow but real growth. In the 1950s and 1960s the state was the principal agency behind a programme of industrialisation more ambitious than Reza Shah's. Tariff barriers and supplementary customs duties were also more widely applied in an attempt to protect domestic industries through the control of imports.[16] State banks and 'mixed' banking institutions (with state, private and foreign capital) played a substantial role in providing finance for private industrial development.

One sector that still lagged far behind was agriculture. The state's support for agricultural development was minute in comparison to its aid to the light manufacturing sector. Even when the state began to increase its support and direct involvement through means such as co-operatives, agricultural production remained far behind that of other sectors, hardly touched by the process of industrialisation.

The tendency towards state capitalism did not mean that the Shah and the Iranian ruling class either intended to, or could, establish a totally state-controlled economy. On the contrary, private industry was encouraged and capitalist firms developed in their hundreds during the 1950s and 1960s, precisely due to the growing role of the state in the overall management of the economy.

One of the most important features of the Iranian economy from the end of the 1950s until the overthrow of the Shah, was the establishment of joint ventures, involving state or private Iranian capital, in partnership with foreign capital. Foreign investment outside the oil sector was minute before the 1950s. After the 1953 coup foreign capital began to move into the non-oil sectors of the Iranian economy. To overcome tariff barriers, to utilise local resources, and to capture part of the domestic market, multi-national firms moved towards direct productive investment. Typical of foreign investment in Iran was the establishment of subsidiaries, almost invariably in partnership with domestic private or state capital. The great majority of such investments were in light manufacturing industries which were, on the whole, geared towards the Iranian market.

By the end of the 1960s, 90 foreign firms had invested in Iran, and by 1974 the number had increased to 183.[17] However, foreign capital investment remained a small proportion of the total. The 1973–78 Plan projected scheduled foreign capital inflow at $2.8 billions, state investment at $46.2 billions, and private (local) investment at $23.4 billions.[18]

The industrial sector of the Iranian economy experienced rapid growth after the inauguration of the Second Plan (1955–62). Between 1960 and 1971, industrial production increased at an average rate of 15.3 per cent.[19] However, this statistical picture could be misleading for Iranian industry started from a very narrow base and, despite its rapid growth, the production of manufactured commodities per head of population remained fairly small in comparison to the advanced countries. The figures for 1963 are: Iran (excluding oil) $28 per head; the USA over $1,000; major Western European countries, between $600 and $800.[20]

The growth in industrial production was almost exclusively due to the so-called 'modern sector' of manufacturing. While the production of large-scale enterprises expanded by 68 per cent between 1963–64 and 1966–67, smaller enterprises (units with fewer than 10 workers) in fact produced 22 per cent *less* in 1966–67 than in 1963–64.[21] Small-scale enterprises, however, were in the majority: 219,000 out of 225,000 enterprises were units employing less than 10 workers in 1972. In 1968, these employed 83 per cent of all workers and in 1977, 72 per cent. Large-scale establishments employed only about 700,000 workers.[22]

Most of the resources for the state economic plans were supplied by oil revenue. For the Third Plan (1962–67) oil revenue accounted for 62 per cent; for the Fourth Plan (1968–72) 63 per cent;[23] this increased to over 80 per cent during the Fifth Plan (1973–78).[24] Indirectly, the oil industry had a very negative effect on Iran: its importance to Western powers ensured that Iran's political life was never wholly free from their intervention and made Iran greatly dependent on the multinational giants. Nevertheless, the flow of oil revenue to the state provided a historically unique opportunity for economic development. Although oil revenue was certainly used to improve the infrastructure, and to subsidise private industrial development, there can be no comparison between the economic development of Iran during the height of the Shah's dictatorship and that of Western industrialised countries. The Iranian economy, in spite of its huge oil wealth, could in no way compete with the major economic powers.

For the state, however, the benefits from oil were enormous. The oil revenue allowed the dictatorship some immunity from socio-economic pressures and from the need to impose severe taxation and fiscal policies.[25] The revenue was crucial in the development of the state sector and in the power of the state over the economy as a whole. It was also vital to the maintenance of the dictatorship. It not only financed the repressive and military structures, it also allowed limited concessions to potentially powerful sections of the industrial working class.

Table 1   Export earnings and oil revenue 1959–60 to 1977–78 ($ million)

Year	Total export earnings	Earnings from export of non-oil goods	Oil revenue	Oil revenue as % of total
1959–60	502	95	335	66.7
1965–66	817	132	608	74.4
1969–70	1,518	231	1,099	72.4
1970–71	1,690	253	1,268	75.0
1971–72	2,734	329	2,114	77.3
1972–73	3,337	403	2,536	75.9
1973–74	6,366	548	5,067	79.6
1974–75	20,922	563	18,671	89.2
1975–76	21,972	447	19,074	86.8
1976–77	24,404	472	20,671	84.7
1977–78	25,989	595	20,926	80.5

Source: Iran Central Bank, *Annual Report and Balance Sheet*, 1971, 1975, 1978.

After the establishment of the consortium, the state's oil revenue increased from 66.7 per cent of total export earnings in 1959–60 to over 80 per cent in the late 1970s (see Table 1). Oil revenue as a proportion of all state revenue increased from 47.9 per cent in 1959–60 to 49 per cent in 1965–66.[26] The contribution of oil revenue to the national budget also grew: from 50 per cent in 1972–73 to 83 per cent in 1975–76.[27]

Military expenditure

A significant proportion of the oil revenue was spent by the Iranian state not on domestic economic development nor on improving conditions for the population, but on financing and equipping its military and repressive forces. There is no doubt that the revenue from the oil industry (especially after the oil price rises of 1973) provided most of the funds spent on armaments, which meant that there was less for the state to invest in the expansion of the means of production. Table 2 shows the correlation between military expenditure and oil revenue.

Table 2 Military expenditure and oil revenue, selected years 1960–77 ($ million)

	1960	1964	1974	1976	1977
Military expenditure	290	323	4,498	6,712	9,430
Oil revenue	335	480	18,671	19,074	20,671

Source: For military expenditure, Stockholm International Peace Research Institute, *Yearbook 1978*, London: Taylor & Francis 1978, Appendix 6A, Table 6A 11, p. 148; for oil revenue as Table 1 above.

By far the most important supplier of arms to Iran was the USA (see Table 3). This exchange of oil for arms from the West[28] was a direct transfer of investible surplus to the West in return for goods which, economically speaking, were totally unproductive. Between 50 and 80 per cent of military expenditure was accounted for by foreign purchases of arms.[29] Between 1970 and 1976 Iran was the largest recipient country in the Middle East of arms from the USA, UK, Italy and Netherlands, with 31 per cent, 26 per cent, 34 per cent and 28 per cent of the total transfer of arms to the third world, respectively.[30] In the same period Iran was the largest arms importer in the third world.[31] This trade was not a simple once and for all purchase of, say, tanks or fighter planes. Especially when buying sophisticated weapons, Iran had to purchase a complete military package. This included technical training, the services of military advisers, spare parts, and so on; in other words, not only the hardware but also the software, which added considerably to the cost.

Table 3 US military sales to Iran, 1950–80 ($ thousand)

	Military sales	
Fiscal year	*Agreements*	*Deliveries*
Cumulative 1950–70	790,525	365,473
1971	354,613	78,566
1972	455,615	214,807
1973	2,133,680	245,293
1974	3,935,069	648,527
1975	1,290,509	985,822
1976	1,558,797	1,890,913
1977	2,760,650	2,416,591
1978	913,494	1,669,142
1979	35,862	1,413,752
1980	0	0
Cumulative 1950–80	14,228,814	9,928,886

Source: R. K. Ramazani, The United States and Iran, New York: Praeger 1982, p. 48

Foreign arms purchases were only one part of military expenditure. There was also production of military equipment in Iran itself: for example, the BAC Rapier SAM missiles under licence from the UK (a joint venture of Irano-British Dynamics). There were similar deals with the USA for Bell helicopters and Hughes TOW anti-tank missiles, assembled at Shiraz in southern Iran.[32] But these were 'sophisticated' weapons; munitions and light weapons factories also produced armaments.

Military expenditure did not end with armaments. During the Shah's dictatorship Iran had one of the largest armed forces in the third world, with around 413,000 men in 1978,[33] and a large network of repressive units: the town and city police, prison staff, the National Information and Security Organisation, SAVAK, and other intelligence and special units. For SAVAK alone, *Newsweek* estimated a full-time membership of 30,000 to 60,000, with perhaps as many as 3 million occasional SAVAK informers[34] all of whom received some form of payment. There was also the cost of extensive bribery and corruption, as well as so-called 'commissions' to middlemen connected to the arms trade, which ran into millions of dollars.[35] Altogether the amount of potentially productive surplus spent on the military and repressive forces was enormous.

The impact of the 1973 increase in oil prices on the state's arms-purchasing ability was great:

> During the entire period from 1950 through 1972 purchase
> agreements amounted to only about $1.5 million, while
> from 1973 through 1977 they rose to a staggering total over
> $11 billion. In the first year after the dramatic increase
> in oil prices, the value of arms transactions amounted to
> twice the total value of all arms contracted during the
> previous 22 years.[36]

By 1976 there was a sharp decline in Iran's investible surplus, from $10.7 billion in 1974 to a projected $4.5 billion in 1976.[37] In the same year the Iranian government announced a budget deficit of $2.4 billion for the coming year, in spite of $20 billion in oil revenue. The reason for this considerable shortfall was given as rising military costs.

Economic waste in Iran went far beyond military expenditure alone. The increasing state bureaucracy, the large number of prestige projects, the huge royal expenditure and so on, all wasted potentially productive oil revenues. This waste of resources was undoubtedly one of the most important reasons for the failure of the Shah's 'economic miracle'.

Growth of the working class

The Iranian working class came from two principal sources: the large mass of landless peasants, and the much smaller social layer active in the handicraft sector of the economy. The impact of European commodities, which ruined many Iranian handicraft establishments, especially in the northern provinces, forced large numbers of Iranians to migrate to the oil towns of southern Russia to find jobs either in the oil industry itself or in other industries linked to it.[38] The oil industry in Iran was also a major employer and by the early 1920s employed over 20,000 Iranian workers, rising to just under 56,000 by 1950 (see Table 4). For a fairly long time it was the biggest and most modern industrial enterprise. More important was the *concentration* of industrial labour in one single industry, which had an enormous influence on the development of political consciousness.

Table 4　Oil industry in Iran, selected years, 1921–50

Year	Production of crude oil (million tonnes)	Workers employed	Rent to the state (£ million)
1921–22	2.3	18,700	0.59
1929	5.5	30,000	1.44
1939	10.1	31,500	3.30
1945	17.1	42,274	5.62
1950	31.7	55,970	16.00

Source: Compiled from Shwadran, *The Middle East, Oil and the Great Powers*, New York: Praeger 1955, table 1; M. Fateh, *Fifty Years of Iranian Oil*, (Persian ed.) Tehran: 1335, p. 434; C. Issawi, *The Economic History of Iran*, University of Chicago, 1971, p. 374.

However, the number of wage-workers really began to grow in the 1950s. There was a major shift of the population away from agriculture during the latter half of this century. At the beginning of the twentieth century agriculture occupied 90 per cent of the labour force; by 1946 the proportion had declined to 75 per cent. In 1966, 46 per cent of the workforce was still in agriculture and related activities;[39] by 1976 this had dropped to only 33.9 per cent.[40] The number of manufacturing workers employed in large-scale enterprises (employing 10 or more workers) increased from 30,000 in 1906 and 198,000 in 1966,[41] to around 700,000 in the 1970s. In 1977 the number of workers in the manufacturing industries as a whole was estimated at 2.5 millions. The total labour force at this time was 10.6 million with 6.8 million employed outside the agricultural sector.[42]

The state sector was the most important area of growth. The number of state employees increased by about 727,000 between 1966 and 1976. About 77 per cent of the labour force in the extractive industries was employed by the state; in the oil industry (after nationalisation) the proportion was 85 per cent and in coal mining 88 per cent. As a result of the state's investment in the engineering and metal industries, the labour force increased by 240 per cent between 1966 and 1976 to 350,000 workers.[43] The number of workers employed in the private sector remained higher than that in the state sector (see Table 5), but as a proportion of the total workforce there was a clear decline (see Table 6).

Table 5 Number of workers by distribution in state and private sectors

	1956	*1966*	*1976*
Private sector	2,245,700	2,635,600	3,038,809
State sector (workers and employees)	450,800	662,600	1,696,049
Total	2,696,500	3,298,200	4,734,858

Source: 'Behrang', *Iran: Le maillon faible*, Paris: Maspero 1979, p. 201

Table 6 Distribution of labour force in state and private sectors (%)

	1956	*1966*	*1976*
All wage workers	100	100	100
Private sector	83	80	64
State sector	17	20	36

Source: As for Table 5, p. 195

Despite its importance as a source of revenue, the oil industry is highly capital-intensive and employs only a small proportion of the Iranian labour force (see Table 7).

Table 7 Sectoral distribution of total labour force 1963–78 (thousands)

	1962–63		*1967–68*		*1972–73*		*1977–78*	
	No.	*Total* (%)	*No.*	*Total* (%)	*No.*	*Total* (%)	*No.*	*Total* (%)
Agriculture	3,672	55.1	3,861	49.0	3,600	40.9	3,200	32.2
Industry	1,372	20.6	1,947	24.7	2,550	29.0	3,300	33.2
Services	1,584	23.8	2,020	25.7	2,600	29.5	3,379	34.0
Oil	36	0.5	46	0.6	50	0.6	60	0.6
Total	6,664	100.0	7,874	100.0	8,800	100.0	9,939	100.0

Source: H. Katouzian, *The Political Economy of Modern Iran 1926–1979*, London: Macmillan 1981, p. 259. (Figures for the labour force in the oil sector include engineering and white-collar staff and management)

Direct employment of wage-workers (excluding staff and management) in the oil industry in fact declined steadily during the 1960s despite the substantial rise in output[44] (see Table 8). The oil industry remained an 'isolated' modern sector. For the mass of the population there was little tangible benefit from the growth of oil wealth.

Table 8   Wage-workers in the Iranian oil industry, selected years 1955–68

Year	No. of workers
1955	48,222
1959	47,984
1960	45,646
1961	39,638
1962	33,765
1963	32,135
1964	31,564
1965	30,732
1966	29,991
1968	27,586

Source: For 1955–66, Bartsch, 'The Impact of Oil Industry on the Economy of Iran', in R. F. Mikesell, *Foreign Investment in the Petroleum and Mineral Industries*, Baltimore: Johns Hopkins Press 1971, p. 254; for 1968, *Iran Almanac*, Echo of Iran, Tehran 1971, p. 334

3. Class struggle, rebellion and the clergy

The social structure of Iran in the late nineteenth and early twentieth centuries was determined by the relationship between five classes: (a) the ruling class, which consisted of the royal family, the high echelons of the state (central and provincial), the tribal chiefs, the religious officials appointed by the state and the landed 'aristocracy' (private landowners); (b) the merchant class; (c) the traditional 'petty bourgeoisie', that is, small traders, shopkeepers, small workshop (handicraft) owners and low-ranking clerics; (d) the urban hired labourers, that is, apprentices, servants, porters, construction workers, etc.; (e) the mass of rural direct producers – by far the largest class.

The social conflicts, struggles and rebellions of the late nineteenth and early twentieth centuries took place largely within the urban areas. The rural population, that is the mass of rural direct producers, were rarely involved. This was not surprising given the self-sufficient and isolated nature of village communities, which were scattered units of production throughout the country. This does not mean that there were no revolts in rural areas, that social conflict was absent or that rural producers lived and laboured in social harmony with their exploiters. What it means is that the rural class struggles were localised; they were settled within particular localities and rarely took on a mass country-wide character. It was in the towns and cities that class struggles involved mass rebellion and, in a few cases, involved every major urban centre. The principal challenge to the established order therefore came from the urban population. In the twentieth century, class struggle emerged principally in the towns and cities (although there were exceptions, particularly in the northern provinces).

Shi'ite Islam as a political force

Religion has been a crucial factor in the consciousness of the population of Iran. It is the most important ideological force for social control; one of the fundamental bases of religion, and in particular Shi'ite Islam, is the submission to authority and the acceptance of a governing elite. Shi'ism came into being as an ideology of protest, and from its birth it acted as a political force. Shi'ism, therefore, proclaims the inseparability of politics and religion.

Shi'ite Islam in Iran provided both a sedative in the face of real suffering, and, at the same time, a protest against oppression, poverty and deprivation. It was this dual function of Shi'ite Islam that provided the basis for its success, especially when there was no viable ideological and organisational alternative. The mosque reinforced that ideology through the traditional institution of charity funds (*zakat*), which provide welfare benefits to the needy. It was the combination of materiality and spirituality that gave the mosque its influential role among the urban masses.

Shi'ism became the state religion with the rise of the Safavid state in the sixteenth century. A Shi'ite clerical hierarchy became an integral part of the centralised apparatus of the state; clerical and state power had become almost completely intertwined.

The reign of the Qajars (1785–1926) was a period of struggle between the court and the clergy, and although the clergy enjoyed considerable influence and power, and took a leading role in social upheavals, they were no longer a fully integrated part of the state structure.

In the early twentieth century the Shi'ite clergy began to lose ground to radical reformers and nationalists, although they still wielded considerable influence. The reign of Reza Shah brought about not only the final separation of the Shi'ite clergy from the state structure, but also a significant diminution in their political weight. In the crisis years between 1941 and 1953 they played no effective political role. The failure of the Tudeh Party and the National Front to take power, and the resultant coup that ousted Mossadeq, rekindled the political spirit of the clergy. Theological circles emerged in Tehran and Qom, and the Shi'ite revivalist movement began. It was not, however, until the 1960s that the clergy reappeared as a major political force.

The clergy can be divided into two sections: a very small minority who were part of the ruling class; and the vast majority who were members of the traditional petty bourgeoisie. The latter were sons of traders, shopkeepers and small merchants of the bazaars. Their connection with the bazaar is, however, not only due to their past family relations, but also due to the financial support the mosque receives from the bazaars.

The strengthening of the state from the 1930s onwards and the trend towards state capitalist development illuminated the common interests of the clergy and the bazaar. The state denied the traditional petty bourgeoisie full participation in the process of capital accumulation. Subsidies and investment opportunities created by the state were virtually unavailable to this class since it lacked access to the higher levels of the state bureaucracy and court. The mosque lost influence over various social, educational and cultural matters, and also saw the trend towards 'Western-isation' as a dangerous threat. Moreover, the crisis of the petty bourgeoisie and merchants meant a reduction in its financial support. The mosque had the organisation and the ideological hold over the urban masses; the bazaar provided the financial aid. Together they united in opposition to the state.

The constitutional revolution

Throughout the nineteenth century one of the major issues of concern to the merchant class and the traditional petty bourgeoisie, an issue which was always present in the conflict between these classes and the state, was that of concessions to non-Iranians. This conflict over foreign concessions was complicated by the struggle between the clergy and the state. The clergy wanted to increase its influence and to establish unity between religious and political institutions. This often meant that many of them would side with the opposition movement against the state. Their self-proclaimed role as the 'guardians' of the Shi'ite community strengthened their resolve to play a 'corrective' role in Iranian society in order to amend the excesses of state officials and ward off the 'infidel aliens' who attempted to divide the community of believers. The clergy therefore often mobilised their resources to check the interventionist inroads of the Europeans in Iran.

Towards the end of the 1890s an underground movement began

with the formation of secret societies comprised predominantly of middle-ranking clergy. By 1904 a number of these secret associations had co-ordinated their activities and, in May of that year, a Revolutionary Committee was formed and a programme of action devised. The ideological framework of these secret organisations was revealed by their stated concern: 'the fear of a threat to Islam from the despotism and tyranny of the government and from foreign powers, notably Great Britain and Russia'.[1] Their goal was the establishment of a code of laws and a system of justice based on the *shari'a* (Islamic law).

In 1905 came an economic crisis caused principally by the disruption of northern trade by the Russo-Japanese war and the 1905 Russian revolution, as well as a disastrous harvest. The already discredited Qajar state was pushed towards its final crisis. The secret societies began to function as 'political parties', becoming increasingly involved in mobilising the urban population. The unrest was fanned by such issues as dissatisfaction with the administration of customs by its Belgian director in April 1905, the victimisation of some prominent merchants, and the murder of an anti-government preacher in July 1906. It culminated in the Shah's capitulation on 5 August 1906 and the convening of a Constituent National Assembly. The battle for the Constituent Assembly was won, but the constitutional revolution was not yet over.[2]

There is no doubt that the clergy played a prominent role in the social upheavals of 1905 and 1906, nor that religion coloured the political and economic issues that dominated the struggle. However, the revolution also involved people radically opposed to the clerical domination of the movement, who had no intention of establishing a political and legal structure wholly based on Islamic law.

The contradictory aims of the radicals and the clergy were bound to emerge sooner or later. With the convening of the Constituent Assembly and the preparation for elections to the National Assembly, the radical elements of the movement attempted to wrest control away from the clergy. However, the clergy had already managed to incorporate Shi'ism into the newly established political structure. This is evident from the adjustments made to the constitution. These included: a supreme committee of leading clergy to scrutinise parliamentary bills and ensure their accordance with Islamic law; a provision that non-Moslems could not be ministers; and the banning of heretical organisations and publications.

In the wake of the constitutional revolution, political organisations, women's groups and radical newspapers appeared throughout the country. A campaign to secularise the constitution and the political structure began with anti-clerical articles in a number of radical papers. In parliament, radicals and liberals began to argue for the separation of secular from Islamic laws. These moves alienated a number of the clergy who saw them as a threat to their traditional role and to their intended influence over the new political structure.

Given this division between the radicals and the clergy, the royalists judged the time to be right for an onslaught on the infantile constitutional order. Civil war began in Tehran in June 1908 when the Cossack Division, under the command of a Russian colonel, attacked the popular volunteer militia guarding the parliament. At the same time, tribal contingents loyal to the old order occupied the central telegraph offices (which were of great importance for communication with the provinces), and mobs attacked and looted the headquarters of radical and constitutionalist societies as well as parliament itself. The royalists won the battle of Tehran, but the war continued in the provincial capitals, and, after this initial victory, the royalists were eventually defeated.

The royalist coup attempt reunited the clergy and the radicals in defence of the constitution, but their ideological divisions could not be forgotten. The mosque and parliament stood side by side rallying the people in the same cause, but not as a unified body. Revolts, armed struggles and strikes in the main provincial capitals (Tabriz in Azarbaijan, Rasht in the north, Isfahan in the centre) soon spread to other urban centres throughout the country, defeating the royalists. These events, and the military victory of the constitutionalists in July 1909, eroded the role of the mosque in the constitutional movement.

The civil war was fought against the background of Anglo-Russian relations. The government in Tehran after the civil war was weak and incompetent, unable to establish internal security or to quash the tribal warfare in the provinces. This lack of security was viewed by both Russia and Britain as sufficient grounds to occupy the country and, at the end of 1911, the two imperialist powers marched their troops into northern and southern Iran. The years to 1917 saw social disintegration and political demoralisation, but the collapse of Russian imperial power rekindled the struggle for liberation and democracy in Iran.

From the Gilan Republic to the rise of Reza Shah

The Gilan Republic
During the Russian occupation of the northern province of Gilan, a small guerrilla force, the Committee of Islamic Unity (popularly known as the *Jangalis* or 'men of the jungle'), harassed the Russian forces. This force was led by a former theology student called Mirza Kuchek Khan, who was a veteran of the civil war and an ex-member of the Moderate Party. The force was made up initially of independent peasants and, to a lesser extent, members of urban petty bourgeoisie.[3] By the end of 1917 the *Jangali* movement had become a major force in the northern Caspian province, controlling most of Gilan.

After the victory of the Bolsheviks in 1917, both British and White Russian forces were using northern Iran as a base for attacking the Soviet state. The struggle of the *Jangali* movement was therefore of prime importance to the Bolsheviks. In May 1920, the Soviet navy landed a Red Army detachment in the port of Enzeli in Gilan. Its objective was to eliminate the British and White Russian forces and to help strengthen the *Jangali* movement against the British-backed central government in Tehran. The Soviet forces brought with them 2,000 members of the Justice Party. The Justice Party had organised trades unions among Iranian workers employed in the Russian oil fields of Baku. Its leadership, who were intellectuals, had worked closely with the Bolsheviks since 1906. After landing at Enzeli, the Justice Party formed an alliance with the *Jangali* movement. In June 1920, at their first major congress, they adopted the title, Communist Party of Iran (CPI).[4] The Republic of Gilan was established.

An attempt by the CPI to spread the revolution by marching on Tehran in August 1920 failed when their forces were defeated. The *Jangalis*, meanwhile, drifted away from the CPI coalition, viewing the land reform programme proposed by the Republic as too radical.[5] After the August 1920 defeat and the departure of the *Jangalis*, the section of the Bolshevik party responsible for the Caucasus, which was headed by Joseph Stalin, brought pressure on the CPI to change its ultra-left programme. At a plenary meeting the party's programme was changed and its First Secretary replaced. The Bolshevik party leadership in Moscow and the Comintern had not officially accepted this change.[6] Nevertheless the new leadership suspended the radical land reform programme in an attempt to bring back the *Jangalis*. By the time the *Jangali* movement rejoined the Gilan Republican government in May 1921, a new and ruthless force had entered Iranian politics – the new military regime of Reza Khan. The Soviet Union signed an agreement with Britain and with the central government in Tehran and withdrew the Red Army. This signalled the beginning of the end of the Gilan Republic. In October 1921 the forces of Reza Khan formally ended the republic and occupied Gilan.

The rise of Reza Shah

It was in an atmosphere of deep political crisis – unrest in Azarbaijan, tribal wars, the Gilan rebellion, mutinies in the gendarmerie – that Reza Khan, a colonel of the Cossack Division, marched into Tehran on the night of 20 February 1921, with a Cossack detachment of only 2,500 men.[7] Martial law was declared in Tehran and Sayyid Ziya al-Din Tabatabai, a former journalist, was installed as Prime Minister.[8] It was not long before Reza Khan, as War Minister, built up the armed forces and increased his own control over them. The defeat of the Gilan Republic and the *Jangali* movement (with Kuchek Khan's head displayed in Tehran) showed the ruthlessness of Reza Khan and helped to strengthen his position. Between 1921 and 1925, he forged the various small military units into a new standing army of five divisions with around 40,000 men.

Reza Khan's consolidation of power, symbolised by his metamorphosis into Reza Shah on 25 April 1926, resulted in the establishment of a monarchical military dictatorship. Reza Shah's reign marked the rise of a modern authoritarian nation state which consolidated its hold on Iranian society by crushing local popular uprisings and eliminating all political opposition. This was carried out in two ways: on the one hand through extreme repression; and on the other, by adapting aspects of the liberal and radical opposition's own programme.

The mosque – which had already lost much of its influence in the political arena but retained fairly strong connections with certain sections of the urban population – was expelled from the political stage. The state took over areas traditionally considered firmly within the religious domain. The establishment of modern educational institutions destroyed the clergy-dominated *madrasa* (school) system; the secularisation of the legal system ended the dominance of Islamic law and the jurisdiction of religious courts; the creation of a Ministry of Endowments severely curtailed the role of the clergy in the administration of religious charitable properties (*vaqf* properties); the establishment of social services (hospitals, public libraries, orphanages) considerably diminished the traditional social role of the mosque; and, finally, the compulsory unveiling of women in public places expressed symbolically the defeat of the clergy and the undisputed power of the modern state.[9] The clergy was so overwhelmed by the advancing power of the state that it did not completely recover until the early 1960s.

The 1953 coup and after

Reza Shah's abdication, forced by the Allied occupation forces in 1941, ushered in a period of intense political regrouping, readjustment and struggle. A multitude of organisations, associations and societies, ranging from the militant to the conservative, grew almost overnight, after 16 years of repression.[10] The ensuing social conflict had a twofold character: the struggle between classes, waged mainly in the urban areas; and the struggle for national liberation in the provinces. The national minorities saw the disruption of the existing political structure as their chance to establish their own independent, or at least autonomous, national government.

The two most important attempts at autonomous government were those of the Azarbaijan and Kurdistan rebels. Both these nationalist movements were initially encouraged and supported by the USSR. In November 1945 the militia of the Democratic Party of Azarbaijan took over the region almost without bloodshed and by 21 November 1945 the rebels controlled most of (Iranian) Azarbaijan. The presence of Soviet troops prevented Iranian military reinforcements from entering the region. On 12 December 1945 the Democratic Party, after negotiating the removal of Iranian troops, established a National Assembly. However, exactly a year afterwards, on 12 December 1946, after an agreement between the USSR and the central government in Tehran, the Iranian army entered Tabriz and put an end to the Azarbaijan revolt.[11]

Meanwhile, in Kurdistan, Kurdish nationalists encouraged by the USSR established a Committee of Resurrection of Kurdistan, commonly known as the Komala. By 1944, the Komala had become the most influential force in northern Kurdistan. In 1945, having attracted a considerable number of activists, the Komala was transformed into the Kurdish Democratic Party; and on 22 January 1946, after a meeting of delegates from all areas of northern Kurdistan, the first Kurdish Republic was proclaimed. Qazi Mohammad, a well-respected religious figure, was elected by delegates at Mahabad as President of the new republic. In March 1946, with the withdrawal of its troops, the USSR abandoned the Kurdish republic and, in December 1946, the Iranian army marched into Mahabad. Most of the leadership were arrested and imprisoned while the President and a few others were sentenced to death and hanged on 31 March 1947.[12]

The struggle of the oppressed and exploited classes in Tehran and other Iranian cities was led by the Tudeh Party. By 1945 the party controlled almost totally the streets of most major towns and cities. It mobilised tens of thousands on several occasions and had undoubtedly proved to be a mass party and a threat to the established order.[13] At the end of 1946, in line with the crackdown on rebellious national minorities, the Tudeh Party was suppressed. When social discontent burst into the open once again, the struggle was cloaked in nationalist ideology and waged against foreign domination. The primary issue had become the nationalisation of the oil industry.

The streets of Iranian cities once more became the setting for bitter struggles in late 1949, when a new political grouping gained prominence. The National Front, led by Mossadeq, won the support of much of the urban population. The Tudeh Party, however, still carried influence in the factories and offices, as well as in the oil industry. The trade unions,[14] controlled by members and sympathisers of the Tudeh Party, were strong and combative, and by 1952 the Tudeh Party had regained its dominance in the streets.

On 19 August 1953 the army moved in to win the battle for the streets; with royalist groups and hired thugs as extra support, the nationalist and Tudeh forces were defeated.[15] The coup, which was organised by the CIA with the full support of British Intelligence, ended a period of fragile democracy. This defeat of the secular political organisations of the left and the radical reformists was a blow from which they never fully recovered. The struggles that followed were increasingly under the influence of the mosque and the Islamic militants.

It was in 1961, with the death of Ayatollah Burugirdi (the supreme chief cleric), that a new figure surfaced as a leading activist in the clerical opposition – Ayatollah Ruhallah Khomeini. Although Khomeini had first promulgated his ideas on the establishment of an Islamic state in a book entitled *Kashf-i Asrar* ('Secrets Revealed'), published in 1944, he remained aloof from the social and political upheavals of the 1940s and the 1950s.

The coup of 1953 had sparked off a crisis in the ranks of the Iranian nationalist movement. The disastrous failure of the National Front and the Tudeh Party to mobilise against the coup had discredited both organisations and had left secular nationalism in disarray. Islam, unscathed by the 1953 events, appeared as a real alternative to the Shah's dictatorship. A number of religious elements broke away from the National Front and formed a new organisation called the Freedom Movement. Meanwhile, the clergy began to reorganise themselves, taking advantage of the political and ideological vacuum created by the regime's systematic suppression of all secular opposition parties.

Between the autumn of 1962 and June 1963, the clerical opposition, headed by Khomeini, outflanked the secular opposition forces, and gathered behind itself a large mass of the urban population. On 5 June 1963 the army ruthlessly crushed demonstrations and riots in Tehran and Qom which had been sparked off by the arrest of Khomeini. This defeat, although important, was not decisive. The demonstrations proved that the clergy could mobilise a sizeable force; that religious ideology and clerical leadership, after an absence of many years, had once again emerged after the failures of left and radical organisations. The streets of the future belonged almost exclusively to the clergy.

Part two:

Crisis and revolution

4. The consolidation of dictatorship

In February 1949, an assassination attempt provided the Shah with a perfect pretext to crack down on opposition forces in an attempt to re-establish the monarchical military dictatorship. Martial law was declared, opposition leaders detained and many newspapers banned. The Tudeh Party was hit hardest with an arrest of many of its members and organisers and, together with the Central Council of the Federated Trade Unions of Iranian Workers and Toilers (CCFTU), it was outlawed. The Shah also turned on parliament, and, by convening a 'managed' Constituent Assembly gained the right, by a unanimous vote, to dismiss the *majlis* (parliament) whenever he wished.

This palace coup was doomed to failure. The Shah had both underestimated the strength of the opposition forces and over-estimated his own support in the country. In a matter of months, various sections of the radical and liberal opposition headed by Mossadeq, some social democratic organisations, a small religious group led by Ayatollah Kashani, and various nationalist groups joined forces to form the National Front. Their platform included two basic demands: democratic rights, and an end to foreign domination symbolised by the nationalisation of the oil industry. The nationalists combined with the organised Tudeh forces in the workplaces and among the youth to ensure a huge response from the urban population against the Shah. In May 1951 Mossadeq became Prime Minister. By May 1953, backed by the National Front and the Tudeh Party, he was able to strip the Shah of the powers he had fought for and gained since 1941.

The first overt attempt to oust Mossadeq occurred on 16 August 1953 when the Imperial Guards, headed by Colonel Nasiri, tried to force him out of office. This attempt was defeated by pro-Mossadeq army officers[1] and soldiers. On 17 August the Shah fled from the country and the streets were filled with jubilant National

Front and Tudeh supporters. However, instead of using this opportunity to defeat the royalists outright and mobilise the people to transform society, Mossadeq ordered the army to clear the streets and establish law and order. Moreover, the Tudeh, which was by far the best organised mass party in the country with an extensive military network, failed to take any initiative and bid for state power.

This gave the royalist forces the opportunity to carry out the plan they had been preparing with the aid of the CIA and British Intelligence. The CIA had, with little difficulty, won over dissidents from the National Front, such as Ayatollah Kashani, who helped, in effect, to neutralise the forces of the traditional petty bourgeoisie. It also recruited a mob from the southern district of Tehran. This mob was organised mainly by leading royalist clerics such as Ayatollah Behbahani and Chelsutuni. It is claimed that about $19 million was spent to oust Mossadeq. On 19 August 1953 the royalist forces, headed by General Zahedi, surrounded Mossadeq's residence, and after a nine-hour battle captured him.[2]

After the overthrow of Mossadeq the Shah returned to Iran in triumph and the armed forces began a long process of consolidation of the power of the Pahlavi dictatorship. The first stage in this process consisted of creating a reign of terror by destroying all opposition and building new organs of power and repression based wholly within the military structure. Mossadeq and many of his leading followers were arrested. With the exception of Fatemi (Mossadeq's Foreign Minister) who was executed, and Lutfi (the Justice Minister) who was murdered, most received fairly lenient sentences. For the semi-clandestine Tudeh Party – clearly seen as the real threat to the Shah's new order – there was no such leniency. Approximately 5,000 of its members were arrested and by 1957 the party's underground network was almost completely destroyed.[3]

Once the opposition had been crushed, a new and more powerful military organisation was created, and a new security organisation appeared on the scene – the National Information and Security Organisation – SAVAK. After the 1953 coup, the military governor of Tehran, General Bakhtiar, and two other officers involved in military intelligence (Colonel Pakravan and Colonel Alavi-Kia) had been given the responsibility of organising a new intelligence and internal security organisation. In 1957 their task was completed and approved by the Shah's parliament; the organisation became a legal part of the state structure. Technical assistance and advisers were provided mostly by the CIA and also by the FBI and Mossad (the Israeli intelligence service).[4]

By the late 1950s the programme to consolidate the power of the Shah was fully operational – at least on the political front – with the expansion of SAVAK networks into almost every aspect of public life, from trade unions to universities, the civil service and industry. The success of the programme was evident not only from the absence of any organised opposition, but also from a decline in the number of strikes. For example, there were 79 strikes in 1953, seven in 1954 and only three in the period between 1955 and 1957.

Having established internal security and a stable political climate, the next task for the dictatorship was to create a social base for itself. The Shah avoided alienating three traditional classes: the landed aristocracy, the merchants and the petty bourgeoisie of the bazaar. The economic policies of the state deliberately refrained from encroaching on the activities of the large landed families, who continued to enjoy considerable economic and social power. To appease the traders and shopkeepers of the bazaar and their traditional close allies, the clergy, the Shah made various religious gestures such as periodic visits to the Islamic holy shrines. He established an 'open door' policy towards senior ayatollahs who enjoyed easy access to the high realms of the state and royal court, and one-time enemies such as Ayatollahs Kashani and Qonatabadi were released from prison. The bazaars were given relative freedom to carry out their own activities and to control their internal affairs.

To create the appearance of democracy, in 1957 the Shah established a two-party system; the intention was to stabilise the political system while giving ultimate control to the Shah and his close allies. Parliament was divided between the National Party and the People's Party, both of which were led by staunch royalist court servants. Elections were held but they were under the strict control of the local police and gendarmerie forces.

The Shah's attempts to establish a social base for his dictatorship received a serious setback in 1960 when an economic crisis shook the state.[5] The combination of deficit financing, the depletion of foreign reserves and a very poor harvest forced the regime to seek emergency foreign aid from the USA and the International

Monetary Fund. Grants and loans were promised on condition that the Iranian government implement a systematic programme of socio-economic reforms. These were agrarian reform, austerity measures including a wage freeze, a reduction of budgeted expenditure, and the shelving of certain over-ambitious infrastructural projects. The economic crisis and austerity measures hit hardest at the working class and the traditional classes of the bazaar. By 1961 the number of strikes had increased from only three in 1955 to 1957 to over 20, of which the teachers' strike was the most significant indicator of the intensity of anti-government feeling, leading as it did to bloody confrontations with the army and the SAVAK. The regime's repressive measures, although seemingly effective, had not eliminated the opposition.

Land reform

Until the beginning of the twentieth century the land system in Iran was bureaucratic rather than feudal. Private ownership of land was weak and tenure was based on a system of land assignment (the *iqta*), which was a grant of one or more villages or their revenue, made by the state to its officials or others. Agricultural production was based on a village community system. Each village community was made up of households with traditional rights to land and water, and those with none. Land assignment was abolished after the Constitutional Revolution by the first *majlis* (parliament), so strengthening private ownership of land. By the middle of the twentieth century a class of absentee landowners composed of members of the royal family, state officials, tribal chiefs, merchants and traditional landowners, enjoyed a great deal of economic and political power. The Pahlavi family were by far the largest landowners. But there were other powerful groups, some of whom owned hundreds of villages. In fact, before the land reform, about 56 per cent of cultivated land was owned by 1 per cent of the population.

The agrarian reform programme, the basic aim of which was to raise output, was put into effect in three phases. The first phase (1962) had two stated objectives: the redistribution of land to those already farming it, and restrictions on the number of villages owned by landowners. The land was to be redistributed according to the hierarchical structures within village communities, with priority going to those who already owned more than just their own labour, such as oxen-owners. Mechanisation and development of plantations, orchards, and so on, were encouraged by their exemption from the redistribution programme.

The objectives of the first phase were formulated on the basis of two important and interrelated considerations. On the one hand was the political aim of agrarian reform – the attempt to silence those social forces that consistently objected to landlordism. On the other was the economic aim – to push through agrarian capitalist development, without disturbing the dominant landlords.

The number of families who benefited from the first phase was less than one-fifth of the total rural population (690,000 families),[6] and many dominant landlords were able to evade redistribution. Families who received land had to repay the value plus 10 per cent over a 15-year period. The result was not to encourage independent peasant farming families, but their eventual dispossession through their inability to repay the credit from the state and the gradual but effective centralisation of landholdings. A farming family which could not meet the necessary payments had two alternatives: one was to sell or return the land to the state or a large landowner; the other, to reduce its living costs to the lowest possible and supplement its subsistence by income from seasonal wage-labour. In fact seasonal migration from poorer areas to the large capitalist farms, towns and cities delayed to some extent the radical uprooting of the rural population, while at the same time hiding the precariousness of its position.

The second phase was designed primarily to increase the number of tenants on the land rather than redistribute the ownership of the land. Altogether $1\frac{1}{4}$ million families received leases on their lands. The objective was to raise agricultural output and satisfy the villagers' demand for land while retaining the confidence of the big landlords who could, under this scheme, still hold on to their property.

The third phase was designed to convert the tenancy agreements brought into being by phase two into ownership by selling the land to the tenant farmers. The result of all three phases, which affected fewer than half the rural families in the country, failed in its main objective of raising output. Over 75 per cent of all those who acquired land had holdings that were too small for even subsistence farming.[7]

In effect, the state had created a peasant class[8] which had never existed before, except as a small minority in the dry farming regions. This was not the growth of agrarian capitalism but it was, nevertheless, a necessary step towards expanding capitalist relations in rural Iran. By creating many small owner-cultivators, while at the same time preventing their viable operation and denying them the possibility of capital accumulation,[9] the state was, objectively, promoting capitalist agrarian production. Had the state really provided sufficient funds and facilities for the peasant smallholder, then it would not have resulted in agrarian capitalism but in the 'petty mode of production' characteristic of European feudalism.[10] The Iranian state's motive in introducing land reform was never to improve the lot of the rural population. On the contrary, its fundamental aims were to free labour from its traditional ties to the land – forming a reserve army available to be exploited by industry as well as capitalist farms – and to accelerate the centralisation of land and the consolidation of ownership into larger units and fewer hands.

Soon after the implementation of the three phases of land reform, the state began to encourage participation in state-controlled co-operative farms, and to promote private and state-owned agricultural companies, all of which were highly capital-intensive and in many cases involved partnership between domestic and foreign business interests. This was the fourth and final push from above. The state had brought about the dissolution of non-capitalist forms of agricultural production and established the power of capital in the countryside. Within two decades the state had become the most powerful economic force in rural Iran.

However, transforming the rural socio-economic structure did not automatically mean agricultural development and in this respect the land reform failed. Iranian agriculture proved incapable of satisfying growing demand and the value of imports of agricultural products rose from $926 million in 1974–75 to about $2,550 million by 1977–78.[11] The increase in oil revenue in the 1970s masked the decay of agricultural production, and delayed its impact on Iranian society.

The introduction of mechanisation, the establishment of capital-intensive farms and the failure of agricultural production to meet requirements, all resulted in the uprooting, after 1973, of much of the rural population, most of whom migrated to the towns and cities and swelled the already large number of urban unemployed. Those who managed to find employment found it merely on a seasonal basis, mostly in the construction industry. A principal political objective of the land reform programme was to create a social base in the rural areas which would support the dictatorship and produce long-term stability.[12] However, its social side effect – the state's creation of a massive army of urban poor – proved to be a major factor in the destabilisation of the regime.

The White Revolution and the Islamic opposition

By 1963 the dictatorship had moved on from its policy of merely wooing the traditional classes and had begun its attempt to create a social base. A six-point programme was presented to the Iranian people: the already implemented land reform; the sale of state factories to finance the land reform; nationalisation of forests; the creation of a rural literacy corps; a new election law to extend the vote to women; and a profit-sharing scheme for industrial workers. This was the beginning of 'the Shah–People Revolution', or White Revolution. To legitimise this revolution a national referendum was held with the predictable result that 99.9 per cent of votes cast were in favour. The most important aspect of this revolution was that it laid the foundation for a state-dominated capitalism in city and countryside.[13]

The land reform programme and the proposed reforms of the White Revolution took much of the steam out of the radical reformist opposition. Although some low-ranking clergy opposed the land reform, the main body of the clergy, and specifically the leadership in Qom, did not oppose agrarian reform. What united the overwhelming mass of the clergy in opposition to the regime was the proposed reform of the election law and in particular women's suffrage, which the clergy proclaimed was contrary to Islamic law. This led to open protest in October 1962, but despite the agitation of many clerics, the mass of the urban population remained unmoved.

It was at this time that Ayatollah Khomeini emerged as a political figure. His shrewd political judgement became clear when he avoided overemphasising the clergy's objection to women's suffrage, equal rights, and so on, but attacked the regime over issues that were clearly unpopular among the mass of the urban population. Between 1962 and 1963 he concentrated on such issues as: military and economic aid from the USA; the granting of immunity from Iranian law to US military personnel;[14] corruption in general and corruption of Islamic beliefs in particular; the rigging of elections and violation of the constitution; the regime's close relations with and sale of oil to Israel; and finally the regime's neglect of the merchants and traders of the bazaar, as well as the workers and peasants.

However, during this period neither the clergy as a body, nor Khomeini, called for the destruction of the dictatorship. Their aim was to further the cause of Islam by persuasion.[15] Khomeini's eventual public denunciation of the Shah on 3 June 1963 established him as the undisputed leader and political spokesperson of the militant clergy and of the urban artisans, peddlers, small traders and shopkeepers. His arrest on the morning of 5 June 1963 sparked off riots and demonstrations in Tehran and Qom, which quickly spread to other major cities like Tabriz, Shiraz, Isfahan and Mashad. The confrontation with the army lasted for three days and an estimated 3,000 demonstrators were murdered on the streets of Tehran alone.[16] This episode signalled a political transformation: the dwarfing of the secular opposition and the advance of the Islamic anti-Shah movement, with Khomeini (who was exiled soon after his arrest) as its most outspoken leader.

After the army had crushed the riots, SAVAK went to work eliminating the religious opposition. Many of the organisers and leaders of the anti-Shah movement were arrested. The dictatorship crushed the opposition before it could become a really effective force. The clerical opposition was unable at this time to rally support among government employees or the industrial working class. The routing of the anti-Shah clergy and their supporters showed the extent to which the regime had consolidated its power.

The June 1963 uprising marked a turning point in the history of the opposition movement in Iran. It not only established Khomeini as the leader of the militant clergy, but also awakened a new breed of young militants who began seriously to question the traditional activities of the old opposition organisations such as the National Front, the Tudeh (Communist) Party and the Liberation Movement. They organised themselves into underground cells and began to raise the banner of armed struggle by means of guerrilla warfare:

on 8 February 1971, a small band of young revolutionaries attacked the gendarmerie station in the village of Siahkal by the Caspian forests in the northern province of Gilan.

There were two main guerrilla groups during the armed clandestine struggle of the 1970s: the Marxist–Leninist People's Fedayeen Guerrilla Organisation and the Islamic group, the People's Mojahedin Organisation. The Fedayeen was initially formed by two separate groups which merged in the course of 1970: the first, founded by a handful of university students who had left the Tudeh Party in 1963, led by Bijan Jazani and Hamid Ashraf; and the second formed by ex-members of the National Front led by two university students, Masud Ahmadzadeh and Amir Parviz Poyan. The Fedayeen were heavily influenced by the Cuban, Chinese, Vietnamese and Palestinian movements.

The Mojahedin was founded in 1965 by six former members of the Liberation Movement. The two leading figures were Mohammad Hanifnezhad and Ahmad Rezai. A few of the original group went to Jordan to receive guerrilla training from the Palestinian Liberation Organisation. Besides establishing guerrilla cells throughout the provinces they formed discussion groups for the reinterpretation of Islam. By the time they began military operations in August 1971 they had developed their own theory of revolutionary Shi'ism. However, in May 1975 a major split occurred in the ranks of the organisation and a Maoist offshoot, later known as the Paykar Organisation, was founded.

This new generation of political activists was convinced that individual or group acts of terror against the Pahlavi regime would eventually lead to the awakening of the masses and a social revolution. However, the events of 1977–78 showed the weakness of guerrilla strategy in generating mass mobilisation.

Bureaucratisation of society

The Shah's regime was based on the militarisation and the bureaucratisation of Iranian society. The regime continued not only to increase the size of the armed forces but also to extend the role of the military establishment into social and economic affairs. Senior military personnel were responsible for running enterprises within the state sector and other major industrial establishments. In almost every factory of any importance SAVAK had its own office; in most cases 'former' officers of the armed forces were responsible for supervising labour relations.

The growth of the bureaucracy, which had begun under Reza Shah, gained momentum after the 1953 coup with the introduction of state economic programmes and plans. By the mid-1960s there were well over 150,000 civil servants; by the late 1970s they had increased to over 560,000. The state bureaucracy accounted for as much as a third to a half of all full-time employees in the urban areas, at least in the major cities. It not only controlled indirectly the everyday life of all Iranian citizens, but had a direct hold over a sizeable section of the urban population.

By the 1970s the White Revolution was in full swing and the state bureaucracy had almost completely replaced the traditional intermediaries between the rural population and the central authority. The state dominated the regulation of water distribution, the exchange of important cash crops, and the determination of prices. In addition, a large section of the rural working population was more directly in the hands of the state bureaucracy through its control over, and administration of, some 89 state farms and 8,500 co-operatives, affecting approximately $1\frac{3}{4}$ million people.

The state's tentacles reached practically every aspect of rural daily life. In the mid-1970s it designed a reorganisation programme to establish 'development zones' and 'non-development zones'; the former would receive subsidies, state credit and assistance, while the latter would be left to stagnate. The aim was to transfer rural working families from the decaying zones to the development zones as wage workers.

In 1975 the process of bureaucratisation became a conscious and deliberate plan. In March, the Shah dissolved the two-party system and created the Resurgence Party, establishing a one-party state. The Shah became the 'Great Leader' and the Resurgence Party the instrument that would complete his 'revolution'. It would establish a 'dialectical' relationship between the masses and the state, combine the best elements of 'socialism and capitalism', eradicate all class distinction, and lead Iran towards a new order, a 'Great Civilisation'.[17]

By June 1975 the Resurgence Party had established women's and youth organisations, had taken over the state-controlled labour unions, and was publishing five newspapers including a 'workers' paper', a 'farmers' paper' and a theoretical journal. It had a forced membership of about 5 million organised into various local branches. It took over, with SAVAK's assistance, all ministries, and closely scrutinised the workings of the mass media, cultural affairs and publishing activities.

The party went even further than this with an active campaign to reorganise the bazaars and the mosque, intending to eliminate their social and economic role in Iranian society. Numerous party branches opened in the bazaars, demanding donations from the bazaaris: shopkeepers, traders and small businesses. The party dissolved the existing system of guilds and created new organisations with Chambers of Guilds controlled by state bureaucrats and non-bazaaris. State corporations were established to import and distribute basic foodstuffs such as meat, sugar and wheat. Both the bazaar and the mosque complained bitterly about these encroachments by the state into their affairs and the lack of assistance to small businesses.

At the same time, the party's campaign against the traditional functions of the mosque was further alienating the clergy and theological students. The party proclaimed the Shah as the spiritual leader of Iran and declared his thoughts and pronouncements to be progressive while denouncing the clergy as 'black reactionaries'. The party also made a number of changes in religious and traditional areas: it replaced the traditional Persian calendar by an Imperial calendar; organised an inspectorate to scrutinise the accounts of the mosque's charitable organisation and those of religious endowments; it gave the right to publish theological materials to the state-controlled Organisation of Endowments; and it created a religious corps to teach the rural population the 'true meaning of Islam'.

On 5 June 1975, on the twelfth anniversary of the arrest of Ayatollah Khomeini, theology students fought the police and gendarmes for three days at the Fayzieh seminary in Qom. Unable to defeat the students, the authorities ordered in a special commando unit. Many students were killed on the spot and about 300 arrested.[18] The incident indicated both the growing alienation of Moslem youth and their defiance. The regime could not dispense with its repressive organisations. The one-party system, rather than establishing stability, increased resentment and dissatisfaction among numerous sections of Iranian society.

5. The social forces of opposition

The bazaar and the modern middle class

The bazaar has for a long time been the main centre of urban life in Iran in spite of overt attempts to diminish its role, and the development of large-scale capitalist production and distribution which inevitably eroded some of its commercial functions. The strength of the bazaar derives from its unique combination of productive and commercial activity with religious and social functions; in totality it provides a communal centre with a life of its own, with its own values, norms and social relationships. The bazaar is a complex, inward looking and highly conservative unity.

The role of the bazaar was based firstly on its financial strength as a commercial centre. Even in the late 1970s it controlled over two-thirds of domestic wholesale trade and accounted for at least 30 per cent of all imports.[1] As a communal centre it also contained the basic elements of political and social power, and rooted in its very structure was the mosque – an institution so closely linked to the bazaar that their separation seemed hardly imaginable.

Concentrated in or connected to the bazaar were the traditional petty bourgeoisie, the merchant class, the mosque and a section of the 'national bourgeoisie', all of whom had suffered under the Pahlavi dictatorship and felt threatened by the growing state machine. The regime's attempts to reduce the power of the bazaar through the creation of a modern banking system, and a distribution system for essential raw materials and foodstuffs, reached its peak in 1976.[2] This onslaught by the dictatorship proved too much for the bazaaris. The dissatisfied merchants and traditional petty bourgeoisie, already united in the complex relations of the bazaar establishment, moved from passive opposition to the regime into activity. As devout Moslems who had always provided funds for the mosque and subsidised religious activity, they saw their salvation in the traditions of Islam.

The middle class – middle-ranking civil servants, lawyers, engineers, university students, academic staff, and so on, totalling perhaps over one million men and women – was also suffering because of the mismanagement of the oil boom. Inflation rose rapidly and an economic crisis deepened. According to government sources, the average cost of imports from the West in 1974–75 rose by 28 per cent.[3] Retail prices increased from an index of 75 in 1972, to 100 in 1974, and 120 in 1976. Foreign economists estimated the rise in retail prices as follows: 15 per cent in 1972; 20 per cent in 1973; 25 per cent in 1974; 35 per cent in 1975; 30 per cent in 1976; and 25 per cent in 1977.[4] By 1975, urban land and property prices were soaring, forcing up the already high rental charges for apartments and houses. The influx of around 60,000 Western military and technical advisers aggravated the middle-class accommodation problem. According to *The Economist* rental charges in residential districts rose by 300 per cent in five years.[5]

The urban poor

As a result of the dictatorship's programme to transform Iran into a 'Great Civilisation', the social composition of the urban population had drastically changed by the late 1970s. The effect of the land reform programme was to undermine the domestic economies of the majority of the rural population. Forced into destitution by the state's plan, a large section of this rural population migrated to the towns and cities in search of employment. The landless producers in the countryside were given 'no protection – no minimum wage, no unemployment relief, no gleaning right on the now-private fields '.[6] Although previously they had received a share of the produce of their village community as a means of subsistence, now, with the breakup of the village community system, they had to purchase their means of subsistence in the market.[7] They therefore had little chance of survival in the rural areas; the cities seemed to provide the only hope. The relatively high wages paid in the urban areas, especially during the early 1970s construction boom, increased the attraction of the cities.[8]

However, not all the uprooted rural newcomers were able to find employment, and for those who obtained temporary work the danger of unemployment was always present. For the vast majority of rural migrants, city life proved just as harsh as village life had been; they had left their village hovels for the shanty towns of the cities. 'Their marginal life on the fringes of society was not really changed by their move to the city – it was merely transplanted from one environment to another'.[9]

One report described the living conditions of the urban poor in one of many such areas in southern Tehran as follows:

> At the south-west corner of Shush Square, an unpaved,
> dirty street leads to a pit, the first in an area known as the
> South City Pits. This enormous hollow measures three
> hectares wide and ten metres deep. Dumped city trash,
> discarded scrap metal, parts of destroyed machinery, old
> cardboard, bones and rotted refuse lie in the middle.
> Outside the pit, a row of houses, loading areas, and tea-houses
> meet the eye. . . . The area inside the pit appears
> uninhabitable. But in truth, cave-like dwellings have been
> dug into the surrounding walls. Used cardboard and paper
> cover the floors. . . . Nearby, similar pits and cave-like
> dwellings are the home of many more people . . . dwellings
> are constructed of discarded scrap metal and cardboard, or
> they have been dug into the ground itself and covered with
> the same materials.[10]

The problem for the dictatorship was not only the great size of this urbanised, uprooted population, nor the extent of their poverty and deprivation, but the fact that they were concentrated together on the fringes of urban society.

The level of political activity was extremely low among the urban poor. In general they brought with them the social consciousness of village life, dominated by Shi'ism. In the absence of legal political organisations the rural migrants found no alternative to religious ideology within urban society. However, they received not only material support and spiritual guidance from the mosque, but, having always respected and feared the authority of God, they now approached the mosque and the clergy with similar attitudes. While they saw the dictatorship as the source of their oppression and deprivation, they saw the mosque as the one organised body that promised a better future.

The working class

The world economic crisis of the 1970s revealed the vulnerability of the Iranian economy, its inability to compete on the world market and its utter dependence on oil. By 1976 the severity of the domestic recession, coupled with high inflation, had drastically reduced the living standards of the working class. Hardest hit were unskilled workers and the new rural migrants whose wage increases barely kept pace with the rate of inflation. The rising cost of accommodation in the large urban centres was the worst problem which the mass of unskilled workers faced in their daily struggle for existence.

Only a small minority of the working class owned their own houses. The state provided some basic accommodation but this was quite inadequate to meet the rising demand for housing. A survey of non-squatting migrant poor carried out in Tehran in 1977 estimated that only around 18 per cent of these newly recruited workers owned their own dwelling units and those that did bore extremely heavy loans. These units lacked basic urban services such as piped water or electricity.[11] The vast majority of the urban wage-earners lived in rented rooms. Many shared rented compounds, an example of which is described as follows:

> Each compound consisted of an old mud-brick caravansary that housed about 40 migrant households. The average household had six members in the one-room shelter. The first caravansary had no running water, no faucets, and no electricity. The few outhouses were shared by all inhabitants. Cooking was done inside the rooms, and water had to be brought in with buckets from a public spigot two blocks away. The second caravansary was less dilapidated and provided the residents with a communal water faucet and an electric light bulb in the yard.[12]

The owner of these compounds was a businessman who, according to the author, made substantial profits from his operations. There were other patterns of rented accommodation. For example, in one part of Tehran were found,

> several rooms . . . with long cloths hanging from the ceiling to the floor for partitioning of the space. Upon questioning,

it became apparent that each partitioned area was rented by the hour to the individual, itinerant migrant labourers who had nowhere to sleep. By paying a nominal hourly fee, the migrants were able to find a few hours of unencumbered rest before their next attempt to search for employment.[13]

Many workers, in desperation, established 'housing estates' outside the official city limits, without water, transport facilities, electricity or other public amenities. Such developments were treated by the authorities as illegal. On numerous occasions city officials, assisted by SAVAK and the police, attempted to demolish these communities. In certain areas some residents were buried under the rubble.[14] On one occasion, in 1977, a householder was beaten to death in an attempt to evict him from his dwelling.[15] In response to these brutal attacks the residents of these 'housing estates' organised themselves to resist eviction and the demolition of their communities. They quickly learned defensive and counter-offensive measures to resist the eviction tactics used by the state officials. One account of a battle between an organised community and the state officials vividly illustrates the rising militancy of these working-class communities:

> We sent the little kids to puncture the tyres of the bulldozers which led their whole army, thus bringing it to a halt and forcing their infantry to invade the area in a disorderly fashion; our women then began to bombard them from the roofs with stones and cobbles which we had already stored up; having thus created disorder, confusion and dismay among the enemy, and inflicted some casualties upon it, we then launched an offensive, and took on the bastards in a pitched hand-to-hand battle. The sons-of-a-whore finally had to run away, leaving some of their machinery and equipment behind. I swear to God, sir, it was really like a Vietcong operation.[16]

Working-class struggles were not confined to such forms of community resistance. Strikes, go-slows, and similar illegal activities were organised at the factory level. Despite the absence of independent trade unions (it is estimated that by 1978 there were over 1,000 trade unions, all of which were state-controlled)[17] certain sections of the working class did manage to exert their influence on wage structures after the 1973 oil price rises. Because of the extreme shortage of skilled labour, wages for skilled workers rose by 30–50 per cent a year.[18] The workers' share programme and profit-sharing scheme of the Shah–People Revolution were attempts to offset wage pressures and encourage greater labour productivity as well as to win over these potentially powerful sections of the working class.

It was clear by the early 1970s that the dictatorship had neither incorporated this class nor raised its productivity sufficiently to implement the economic expansion programme. By 1976 both the business community and the state bureaucracy were extremely concerned at the high level of wages and the low level of labour productivity. In May 1976 the then Labour Minister, Moini, stated in a speech to the Third Iranian Labour Congress that 'workers should strive to work harder, improve their skills and raise productivity in an effort to repay their debts to the Shahanshah'.[19]

The increase in strikes, go-slows and workers' sabotage in the 1970s[20] was provoked by the attempted intensification of labour exploitation and by the spiralling rate of inflation. The number of strikes reported rose from a handful during 1971 to 1973 to as many as 20 or 30 per year in 1975.[21] The vast majority of these were at the individual factory level. The workers' grievances were on the whole concerned with economic issues such as hours of work, bonuses, wages and particularly overtime. As the *Financial Times* reported in 1977: 'Where employers tried to impose restraint they have frequently found a well organised labour force capable of go-slows and strikes (even though illegal) which by and large have succeeded.'[22]

In the strategically important industries like oil, strikes and industrial disruptions were generally very short and, on the whole, successful. Workers in these industries and skilled workers in general could not easily be replaced and so were in a stronger bargaining position than others. In some cases – for example, the strikes in the oil industry in August and October 1973 and March 1975 – the regime made concessions rather than risk a major confrontation with the workers. In other cases, like the 1974 strike at the Mashin Sazi Factory in Tabriz, one of the largest factories in Iran, the 800 striking workers were dispersed by the police and 25 of the younger workers sent off to do military service. A further

100 workers were sacked but eventually, because of the shortage of skilled labour, most of them were rehired.[23]

Many strikes, however, were brutally suppressed by SAVAK, the uniformed police or the army. For example, in May 1974, at the Khavar factory a strike was broken by the intervention of the army and two workers were killed.[24] In September 1974 SAVAK intervened during a strike and occupation at Irana Ceramics in Tehran, which resulted in the death of four workers.[25]

Between 1975 and 1977 there were reported some 60 major strikes, protests or occupations. Less than a third were even partially successful, and about 21 were dealt with violently.[26] The political and economic situation in Iran during the late 1970s was such that no strike or other industrial action was likely to be allowed to continue for any period of time.[27] Therefore, the demands of the workers were met promptly, either by repression or by concessions granted to avoid further disruption and perhaps loss of skilled labour.

Although the working class became more militant in the late 1970s, both at the community level and in individual factories, there existed no organised labour movement in Iran. Because of the repression and ruthlessness of the dictatorship, the fragmentation of the working class, and the backward nature of Iran's economic development, the self-organisation and self-development of the working class had never fully matured, in spite of its size and economic power. Only a small proportion of the working class was concentrated in large industrial units, and there was a continuous influx of new recruits from the rural areas. As a result the level of political consciousness among Iranian workers remained fairly low. During the upheavals of 1978 and 1979, deprived of any independent political or organisational experience, or any organisational leadership from Stalinist, reformist or guerrilla groups, Iranian workers tended to follow the lead of the mosque and the clergy rather than leading the struggle themselves.

6. From protest to revolution

As late as the mid-1970s, the Pahlavi dictatorship seemed indestructible, despite the deepening economic crisis and the social unease among the oppressed and exploited classes. The stability of the regime seemed unquestionable given its military apparatus, its internal and external security network, and its income from oil. After the establishment of the one-party system which had taken over many aspects of social and cultural affairs, and some 15 years of state-initiated reforms, it seemed that the dictatorship had at last achieved its aim of consolidating its power by creating a social base for itself.[1] This was the view not only of most observers but, perhaps more important, the view of the majority of the ruling class and of the Shah himself.

It was an illusion that led the regime and its foreign supporters to imagine that both the economic crisis and the underlying social tensions could be overcome. They tried to do this in two ways. One was to use economic austerity measures to control inflation, at first by a well-orchestrated campaign against so-called profiteers and later, this having failed, by drastically cutting civilian (but not military) expenditure and engineering a recession. The other was to allow a gradual 'liberalisation' to release some of the social tension.

Relaxation of police controls

For a long time Iranian students and political exiles in the West had waged a propaganda campaign against the Pahlavi dictatorship, and, in the mid-1970s, this began to show results. One of the major aims of the opposition in exile was to bring the brutal practices of the Shah's regime to the attention of the public, the press and independent organisations in the West. In early 1975 Amnesty International declared that Iran was one of the world's 'worst violators of human rights'; in January 1975 the *Sunday Times* ran a series of exposés on the Shah's secret police, SAVAK, and its use of torture and murder.[2] It was not long before the International Commission of Jurists, based in Geneva, publicly deplored the regime's systematic practice of torture and its violation of the basic civil rights of Iranian citizens.[3]

This exposure of the dictatorship's repression and abuse of human rights gathered momentum, especially when US Presidential candidate Carter championed the cause of human rights and mentioned Iran in his election campaign. The mass media, US Congressional subcommittees, and human rights groups started to pay attention to the repressive practices of the Shah's regime. External pressure was mounting, and, with the election of Carter to the White House, the Shah began to relax police controls slightly.

This was an important political error, founded on the illusion that the Shah's reforms had worked, that the regime had created a social base for itself, that the opposition was neither organised nor strong enough to challenge the power structure, and that gradual liberalisation would, sooner or later, pacify the opposition.[4] The Shah himself, and his supporters, actually believed that the regime was popular. As one commentator put it: 'decades of propaganda had managed to fool the ruler if not the ruled'.[5]

The relaxation of police controls began in early 1977 and, in February, the Shah ordered an amnesty for 357 political prisoners. During the following months the regime allowed the International Commission of the Red Cross to visit some 3,000 prisoners in 20 prisons across the country, and allowed Western lawyers into a military court to observe the trial of 11 political dissidents. In a private meeting with an Amnesty International representative the Shah promised to improve prison conditions; and in another private audience given to the International Commission of Jurists' representative, he agreed to reform court procedures in order to protect the rights of political offenders.

In June 1977, the Resurgence Party was ordered to allow open discussion of political issues and constructive criticism of internal party functioning and ideas. To show his goodwill, the Shah dismissed Premier Hoveida who had been in office for over 12 years and replaced him with Jamshid Amuzegar on 7 August 1977. Amuzegar was apparently selected by the Shah for two main reasons: he had 'good friends' in the USA[6] and he was believed to have the ability to handle the economic crisis.

The Carter administration did not inaugurate a sudden sharp break with its predecessors' practices[7] as far as Iran was concerned. Carter's election speeches on human rights were not reflected in his deeds; there was no significant pressure from his administration for an outright liberalisation of Iran's political structure. Although the Carter administration discussed arrests and torture with the Shah, no threats were made and support was not reduced.[8] This does not mean that the Carter administration was opposed to political liberalisation as a long-term goal. On the contrary, this was one part of its two-pronged approach: 'It aimed at "political liberalisation" by the Shah, with US support for the Shah presumably toward that goal.'[9] However, what was important in the events to follow was that both the Shah and the opposition believed that the USA might act for human rights.[10] This belief resulted in a slight relaxation of repression by the Shah, and encouraged the opposition to raise its voice.

The protest of the intelligentsia

The first voices to be heard at this time were those of the intelligentsia (although there had been a number of opposition activities a couple of years before). In May 1977, their protest surfaced with a declaration in the form of an open letter to the royal court. Signed by 53 lawyers – many of them former Mossadeq supporters – it accused the regime of interfering in judicial procedures and announced the foundation of a commission to monitor and protect the judiciary. This was followed in June by two open letters. One was signed by 40 writers and addressed to the Prime Minister, calling for an end to censorship and declaring the revival of the Writers' Association, which had been banned in 1964. The second, addressed to the Shah himself, was signed by three prominent leaders of the National Front (Bakhtiyar, Foruhar and Sanjabi). It accused the regime of ruining the economy, especially agriculture, and of violating human rights and the 1905 constitution. It demanded the abolition of the one-party system, the release of political prisoners, and freedom of the press and of assembly – in short, constitutional government.

During the summer and autumn of 1977 the protests of the

intelligentsia gathered momentum. Committees, groups and associations of various kinds were formed: the Iranian Committee for the Defence of Freedom and Human Rights; the Association of Iranian Jurists; the Group for Free Books and Free Thought; the National Organisation of University Teachers, and so on. Even the merchants and traders of the Tehran bazaar formed their own Society of Merchants, Traders and Craftsmen to oppose the practices of the Resurgence Party. Theology students established the Educational Society of Qom and demanded the return from exile of Ayatollah Khomeini among other measures.

These developments encouraged the re-emergence of former political opposition parties and the publication of political newspapers. The National Front was revived by Sanjabi, Bakhtiyar and Foruhar under the new title of Union of National Front Forces; its paper was called the *Khabarnameh* ('Newsletter'). Bazargan also revived his Liberation Movement. The Tudeh Party surfaced with cells in Tehran, Abadan and Rasht, and published the newspaper *Novid* ('Good News'). All these parties were concerned with making the existing political structure more democratic, that is, a return to the constitutional system of 1905–09.

This middle-class, respectable and peaceful opposition was to change drastically by the end of autumn 1977, when, once again, the streets of Iran became the main political stage. The turning point came in November at the tenth session of a peaceful poetry-reading organised by the Writers' Association and the Iranian–German Cultural Society at the Aryamehr University, with an audience of something like 10,000 to 15,000 people. An attempt by the police to stop the session met with an angry response. Thousands marched on to the streets and clashed with a well-prepared force of police and SAVAK agents. One student was killed, 70 were injured and 100 arrested.[11] A number of student demonstrations followed and Tehran university closed in protest. Many other universities soon followed suit and went on strike in solidarity, with further demonstrations and arrests.

These protests by the intelligentsia were, however, only the most vocal and well-publicised opposition activities. Between June and October 1977 two important developments took place. The first was a head-on collision between 'city limits' dwellers and city officials and armed agents. In June 1977 the regime served eviction notices on thousands of unskilled workers, urban poor and dispossessed people living in shanty towns and self-made 'housing estates' on the outskirts of Tehran: 'The eviction would remove 50,000 landless peasants [sic], urban poor, the maimed, the blind and aged people living in the "city limits" dwellings.'[12] Bulldozers soon followed, along with violent attacks by the police and SAVAK. Between June and August there was a series of assaults on these 'city limits' dwellers who daily became more militant and improved their defensive tactics. The process came to a head on 27 August when about 50,000 dwellers supported by students and some clerics demonstrated and attacked the police, forcing them to retreat and the government to suspend temporarily its eviction plans. This victory boosted morale and proved to be valuable experience in organising resistance to the regime. The second development was a series of violent acts of sabotage by angry young workers from July to mid-October. Something like 130 factories were partially destroyed by fires started by workers.[13] On 24 July, for example, the General Motors assembly plant in Tehran was set on fire by the workers, of whom 300 were arrested.[14] During the summer of 1977 a series of strikes was provoked by the cancellation of special benefits, wage cuts and the regime's austerity measures.

The clergy

The clergy and the mosque, meanwhile, were never absent from the scene. The militant clergy (followers of Khomeini) had nurtured a well-organised network of cadres throughout the country, especially in the urban centres. They had used their freedom to preach religious sermons as a means to perpetuate a high level of religious consciousness. Through passion plays staged on days of religious mourning, they had on numerous occasions 'rehearsed' the social drama of fighting tyranny. They had linked the Karbala paradigm – the intense, emotional story of Hussein, the third Shi'ite Imam – with the struggle against the Pahlavi dictatorship. One writer describes it as:

> the reference point for almost all popular preaching . . . Its focus is the emotionally potent theme of corrupt and oppressive tyranny repeatedly overcoming (in this world) the steadfast dedication to pure truth; hence its ever-present,

latent, political potential to frame or clothe contemporary discontent.[15]

It was in the month of Muharram (which fell in December 1977 and January 1978) that religious students, the militant clergy and the mosque again entered the struggle. A planned commemoration of the fortieth-day memorial of the death of Khomeini's son – who had died at the end of autumn 1977 – was banned by the regime. Khomeini, still in exile, rather than making any pronouncement on his son's death, reiterated his call for the overthrow of the Shah and the re-establishment of the 1905 constitution. The regime's response to this call was a blatant attack on Khomeini and the clergy in the semi-official newspaper, *Ettela'at*. An article reportedly encouraged by the Shah himself,[16] written under a pseudonym by the Information Minister Daryush Homayoun, labelled the clergy as 'black reactionaries' and charged Khomeini with being a British spy receiving funds from England and with being really a foreigner ('this Indian Sayyed') who had written love poems of an erotic nature.[17]

This article was the spark that ignited a series of explosive events which shook the Pahlavi regime to its foundations. Theology students in Qom staged a massive demonstration. The bazaar closed down in protest. The streets of Qom saw violent confrontations between some 4,000 religious students and sympathisers, and the police. In the ensuing two days of fighting some 70 people were killed[18] and over 500 injured.

The incident at Qom marks the point from which the religious opposition, under the leadership of the militant clergy and the mosque, moved towards an Islamic revolution and an inevitable collision with the forces of the state.

Ayatollah Shariatmadari (a leading moderate, an advocate of the proper implementation of the 1905–09 constitution and the supreme religious authority inside Iran) declared the Shah's regime to be non-Islamic, with the backing of 120 other important clerics.[19] The dead became martyrs; each burial procession an event for mass protest; each fortieth day (after a death) – traditionally an important time for mourning the dead – was a date for a mass demonstration which in almost every case turned into a riot.

The fortieth day of the Qom martyrs fell on 18 February

1978. The clergy called upon the whole population to observe this fortieth day by attending prayers at the mosques and staying away from work. The bazaars closed, schools and universities were shut down, but not all workplaces observed the day of mourning. Peaceful demonstrations took place in 12 cities. In Tabriz, the capital of Azarbaijan, small groups of demonstrators began to march through the streets and, as the day progressed, they were joined by other groups of people attending mosques. The anti-regime slogans of the crowd reverberated across the city. What was intended as a peaceful demonstration turned to violence when a young protestor was shot dead by the police. The crowd, outraged at this act, marched on police stations. Many demonstrators armed themselves with stones, sticks, molotov cocktails and other such weapons.[20] The police either fled or turned a blind eye[21] as, for 36 hours, Tabriz was taken over by the seething crowd (estimated at around 40,000).[22] There were attacks on 73 banks, a number of luxury hotels, liquor stores, cinemas (showing sexually explicit films), police stations and Resurgence Party offices. Hardly any private individuals were attacked; there was little or no looting. The riot was a political gesture of defiance and the crowd chose its targets consciously, attacking only symbols of the long years of repression. On the second day the army entered Tabriz with armoured troop carriers, tanks and helicopter gunships; the streets became a battle ground: 'There was a torrent of blood running on the streets.'[23] According to various estimates, between 100 and 300 people were massacred in several hours of fighting, and hundreds of militants were arrested.[24] Tabriz was effectively placed under martial law and troops remained on the streets until March. The Shah dismissed the governor-general, and publicly reprimanded the Tabriz SAVAK.[25]

Religious and secular opposition leaders called for demonstrations to honour the fortieth day of the martyrs of the Tabriz massacre. Meanwhile, however, news had reached the opposition of a hunger strike by some 200 political prisoners at Tehran's notorious Qasr prison. On 15 March, despite publicity given to the strike by the Iranian Committee for the Defence of Freedom and Human Rights, the prison authorities and SAVAK ended the strike by severely beating the fasters.

The fortieth day of the Tabriz massacre fell on 29 March and for three days the streets of some 55 urban centres were filled with large memorial processions. In Yazd, Isfahan, Babol and Tehran, these turned into riots which were not unorganised and spontaneous, but well-organised, violent political demonstrations. Once again the symbols of oppression – police stations, state party offices, luxury hotels, banks and statues of the Shah – bore the brunt of the crowd's anger.

In Yazd, the three days of violence started at a bazaar mosque after a fiery speech by a recently released militant preacher. Some 10,000 mourners marched on to the streets heading for the police station, shouting slogans such as 'Death to the Shah', 'Long live Khomeini', and 'Khomeini is our leader'. Before they could reach their target, however, they were met by a cordon of armed riot police firing indiscriminately into the crowd, injuring many hundreds and killing at least 120 demonstrators.[26]

The militant clergy was rapidly gaining ground; the whole movement was being directed by the mosque which used every funeral procession to raise the level of hatred for the Pahlavi dictatorship. Ayatollah Khomeini (still in exile) and the moderate Shariatmadari – as well as other religious leaders – called for a third fortieth-day memorial on 10 May. Memorial processions turned into organised demonstrations and disturbances in at least 34 urban centres.[27] The extent of the demonstrations, riots and violent confrontations with the authorities forced the Shah to cancel his planned visit to Eastern Europe. Troops were ordered on to the streets in many parts of the country; in Tehran about 2,000 troops surrounded the bazaar to break up a gathering outside the main bazaar mosque.

Qom braced itself for a clash which became inevitable when the army was brought in to quash disturbances after 10 hours of conflict. The city's electricity was cut off by the authorities and troops attacked demonstrators in the side streets of Qom, sending volleys of bullets into gathering crowds. In one incident, a number of soldiers chasing a group of demonstrators invaded Ayatollah Shariatmadari's house and shot dead two theology students who allegedly refused to shout 'Javid Shah' ('long live the Shah').

Terror and concessions

The regime was severely shaken by such strong and widespread protests. A complex strategy, which included promises and concessions as well as covert SAVAK activity, seems to have been devised to quell the social unrest. Two organisations – the terror units of 'commandos' and the Underground Committee of Revenge – were specially created by SAVAK.[28] Their task was to intimidate the opposition leadership physically, to create an atmosphere of terror, and to discredit the opposition. Threatening letters were sent to prominent human rights campaigners; well-known members of the opposition were attacked and beaten up; in one case two members of the Writers' Association were kidnapped and badly beaten. The offices and homes of a number of leaders such as Sanjabi, Bazargan, Foruhar and Matin-Daftari were bombed. The terror units also attacked Baha'is and other religious minorities to discredit the militant religious opposition. Many naive propaganda tactics were used to discredit the leaders of the opposition. For example, leaflets were distributed accusing National Front leaders of being agents of American imperialism and religious militants were accused of being associated with 'communists' and the USSR.

The Resurgence Party created its own vigilante groups who operated under an umbrella organisation entitled the Resistance Corps. Their members were recruited from the police force and operated in civilian clothes disguised as workers and students. Their task was to attack meetings organised by the opposition, especially those organised by the mosque, students, the National Front and the Writers' Association. 'In one such attack, the Resistance Corps, pretending to be irate workers, seriously injured 30 people who were celebrating a religious festival in the private gardens of a National Front leader.'[29]

At the same time the regime attempted to win over the moderate elements of the clergy, the bazaaris and the secular opposition. For example, the government made a public apology to Ayatollah Shariatmadari for the attack on his home; promised the Qom clergy that the Fayzieh seminary would be allowed to reopen, and banned sexually explicit films. To please the bazaars, it ended the war on 'profiteers', freed shopkeepers imprisoned for alleged 'profiteering' and recognised the Society of Merchants, Traders and Craftsmen. To appease the moderate leaders of the secular opposition, the Shah promised that the forthcoming parliamentary election would be '100 per cent free' and instituted a few minor changes. For instance he ordered his relatives to end their business activities and issued a code of practice for the royal family; the infamous General Nasiri, head of SAVAK since 1965, was replaced by General Moqadam;[30] and press censorship was slightly relaxed.

The fortieth-day memorial of the massacre of demonstrators on 10–12 May was conducted, according to the wishes of Ayatollah Shariatmadari, peacefully. For two full months during the early summer of 1978 the streets were surprisingly silent. The regime's strategy of terror, conciliation and promises seemed to have worked. The year of protest seemed to be over, and the regime appeared confident that the crisis would not lead to revolution. Premier Amouzegar proclaimed in June 1978: 'the crisis is over'. But beneath the air of calm the storm clouds of revolution were growing. The crowds were temporarily off the streets but they would not be for long.

The working class and urban poor enter the struggle

Until the summer of 1978 the struggle against the Pahlavi dictatorship was mostly the protest of the intelligentsia, traditional bazaaris and the petty bourgeoisie. The participants, with few exceptions, were drawn from the universities, the seminaries and the bazaars. The upheavals from October 1977 to June 1978 rarely involved the industrial working class, the urban poor or the newly recruited 'migrant' workers; and only seven major strikes were reported during this period.[31]

By mid-summer 1978 the situation had drastically changed; the number of strikes rose sharply as the economic crisis deepened, real wages fell and the number of unemployed increased.[32] As the regime's campaign against high wages and low labour productivity took effect, the working class entered the arena of struggle.

The first wave of strikes in June 1978 was still mainly concerned with economic issues, especially bonus payments, overtime and wages. Electrical workers in Tehran and the southern cities struck over the cancellation of their annual bonuses. Water workers and some industrial units in Tehran also stopped work. From July to September, the number of strikes multiplied. In Abadan, 600 sanitation workers demanding 20 per cent wage increases, annual bonuses and a health insurance scheme went on strike in early July. Towards the end of July, over 1,750 textile workers at

Behshar struck over wages; they questioned the role and nature of the state unions and demanded free elections for union representatives. In August a number of strikes took place in Tabriz, the most important of which was that of 2,000 or so workers at the main machine tool factory. The strikers stayed out for two weeks demanding higher wages, annual bonuses, as well as better housing and social conditions. In September workers came out in a number of major strikes in Tehran, in the province of Fars and in Khuzestan, particularly the city of Ahwaz; car assembly plants, machine tool factories, paper mills all became scenes of struggle.

Although the factory floor had begun to articulate its own demands, there was as yet no national movement of workers; nor was there, at this stage, a fusion between the workers' demands and the political demands of the intelligentsia. However, the working class was, for the first time after a long period of forced apathy and passivity, growing stronger and more confident day by day.

The silent masses of the urban poor, the unemployed, 'migrant' construction workers and state employees, who had previously (with a few exceptions) refrained from taking part in the struggle against the regime, also began to join the demonstrations. On 22 July 1978, a funeral procession for a local cleric in the north-eastern city of Mashad drew a large number of workers, unemployed and urban poor. The procession turned into a violent demonstration as some of the participants attacked the police with stones and other objects. The police responded by firing indiscriminately into the crowd, killing 40 people. The summer lull was over.

The Mashad massacre sparked off further demonstrations and violent confrontations as large memorial services, held in almost all the major urban centres, turned into bitter clashes with the agents of repression. The militant clergy again took the initiative as funeral processions, memorial services and fortieth-day commemorations became the vehicle of mass mobilisation. Fiery preachers used every 'sermon' to further their political message of hate for the regime, to relay Khomeini's declarations and pronouncements, and to agitate for greater upheavals.

The month of Ramadan (August) destroyed, once and for all, the illusion that 'the crisis was over'. The regime was taken aback by the number of people who turned to the streets to show their anger and hatred in violent demonstrations and bloody skirmishes.

More important was the change in the social composition of the crowd. As the people assembled, it became obvious that these gatherings were no longer only of students and political activists, but that the demonstrations were being swelled by groups from shanty towns, illegally established housing estates, the unemployed and the self-employed, street-corner pedlars, migrant construction workers, as well as state employees and industrial workers.

During 9–17 August there were continual demonstrations in many cities and towns; the most violent occurred in Tabriz, Mashad, Ahwaz, Shiraz and Isfahan. In Shiraz, an American university teacher describes the situation thus:

> things had moved away from the university and into the Shiraz community. There was an incident at Shahe-Cheragh. A plainclothes man tried to arrest someone in the courtyard for distributing literature. He was surrounded by the crowd and badly beaten. In the course of it he summoned other police, or the army. People were killed. It may have been two, it may have been 20. In any case, it was serious.[33]

In Isfahan, for the first time, street clashes turned into armed skirmishes. As the crowd invaded the streets, some angry demonstrators armed themselves with pistols. Many parts of the city were taken over after some 18 hours of rioting. The crowd even managed to release 'a highly respected ayatollah who had just been arrested'.[34] It took two days of street battles, additional army contingents and the massacre of over 100 demonstrators for the regime to regain its hold over the city. During the two days of fighting SAVAK, assisted by the army, terrorised the city population; anyone on the streets was a potential target; many individuals were battered and clubbed; homes and shops were ransacked. This was one of the ugliest incidents since the beginning of the protests.

The Abadan tragedy

As the regime braced itself for the next round of fortieth-day memorial demonstrations, a tragedy at Abadan shook the country. At 9.45 p.m. on 19 August – which coincided with the twenty-fifth anniversary of the restoration of the dictatorship in 1953 – a cinema in a working-class district of the oil town of Abadan was gutted by fire. A total of 410 men, women and children were burnt to death, deliberately locked inside the burning building for 40 minutes. The official *Pars* news agency (PANA) promptly broadcast the regime's view that this despicable act of arson, like other recent attacks on cinemas and bombings, was the work of 'extremist Moslem reactionaries' protesting at the twenty-fifth anniversary of the 1953 coup and the Shah's 'modernisation policies'. However, all the evidence – accounts from eye-witnesses and survivors, the location of the cinema, the film being shown, the fact that on previous occasions only empty cinemas with programmes of sexually explicit films were attacked or bombed – points the finger at SAVAK. A survivor, who was in the lobby of the cinema buying a sandwich for his child when the fire started, states:

> I suddenly found myself surrounded by fire and parts of my shirt caught on fire. A few people who were escaping pushed me out with them, and in a great shock and astonishment, I watched the doors being locked on the people inside the theatre and I heard a voice saying, 'terrorists are in the theatre, do not open the doors'; I don't know how it happened.[35]

Although no one knows exactly 'how it happened', for thousands of relatives and other people it was clear that SAVAK and the police were to blame. Ten thousand relatives and supporters attending a mass funeral forced the police and municipal officials to leave the cemetery, and began a march through the town shouting: 'Burn the Shah', 'The Shah is the villain' and 'End the Pahlavi tyranny'. The tragedy sparked off six days of street battles between the police and demonstrators.

More concessions

The end of Ramadan brought more agitation, more demonstrations and more violence. The message of the crowd, encouraged by the uncompromising stance of Khomeini and the militant clergy, was clear: the Shah must go; the Pahlavi dictatorship must end. Even at this stage there was no question as to who led the masses: not the liberals or the left but the clergy and the mosque. Moreover, every development increased the hold of the militant clergy over the mass movement, leaving little room for self-activity or self-organisation. The mosque provided the cadres and the ideology;

the merchants of the bazaars, the financial support; and, increasingly, the urban poor, the dispossessed, the lumpen proletariat and the working class provided the army.

The government, shocked and worried, attempted to calm the situation by granting more concessions. On the anniversary of the 1905 Constitutional Revolution, the Shah promised that all political parties, with the exception of the Tudeh Party, would be free to campaign and participate in the forthcoming parliamentary elections. As a gesture of goodwill, 261 political prisoners were released and the regime lifted the censorship on news and allowed industrial disputes and the activities of opposition organisations to be reported. The Shah dismissed Amouzegar as Prime Minister and brought in Sharif Emami, whose relations with some of the high-ranking ayatollahs were good, and who was given full authority to negotiate with the moderate clergy.

However, the concessions were too little and too late. The Shah, his new Prime Minister and his other supporters hoped and worked for the impossible. They were blind to the graffiti on the walls of the side streets, to the bloody hand-prints where wounded protestors marked the places where tens and hundreds had been gunned down by the army or SAVAK. It was useless to woo the moderate clergy or the secular opposition. The celebrations of *'Ayd-i Fetr* (the day ending the Ramadan fast) proved this. As people poured on to the streets of every town, and over 100,000 left the main mosques of Tehran to assemble at the Shahyad Square, their message came across loud and clear. One of the most frequently shouted slogans was: 'We want Khomeini back.' It was not the moderates but the *militant* clergy who were in charge, with Khomeini as their unquestionable leader:

> Throughout the 1977–78 period Khomeini's popularity grew. . . . For the urban poor Khomeini and his words were supreme guides, and as revolutionary anger, enthusiasm, and activity grew, Khomeini's refusal to make any compromise with the monarchy and his implication that problems could be solved by a return to Islamic ways had increasing appeal for the Moslem masses.[36]

For three days following the *'Ayd-i Fetr* celebrations, crowds continued to take to the streets. The urban poor swelled the ranks of bazaaris, students, members of the middle class and radical activists. This was in spite of the call for restraint from the moderates of the opposition, and more important, despite the regime's ban on outdoor assembly and meetings. By 7 September 1978 the main streets of Iran's towns and cities witnessed mass demonstrations not by thousands or tens of thousands but by hundreds of thousands of people. In Tehran wave after wave of demonstrators – over half a million – poured on to the streets shouting: 'Death to the Pahlavis', 'Yankees go home', 'The Shah is a bastard', 'Islam is our guide, Khomeini is our leader' and 'Independence, freedom, Islamic republic'.

Martial law and 'Black Friday'

The size of the multitude, its social composition, its disciplined character and radicalised slogans, as well as its continuous appeals to rank and file soldiers, finally convinced a section of Iran's rulers and the Shah himself that things had gone too far; it was time to act forcefully and decisively. On the night of 7 September martial law was declared in the capital and 11 other major towns and cities, with a curfew from 9 p.m. to 5 a.m. In Tehran, General Oveissi – whose role in crushing the 1963 upheavals had earned him the title 'the butcher of Tehran' – was appointed military governor, and warrants were issued for the arrest of a number of prominent opposition leaders. The state, backed by the full might of the armed forces, was confronting the mosque with its as yet unarmed army of workers, urban poor, students, women and teenagers.

On the morning of Friday 8 September thousands of people defied martial law and a ban on marches and swept on to the streets, even though there had been no call from religious leaders. A violent confrontation had become inevitable. A crowd of several thousand gathered in Jaleh Square, in eastern Tehran. They had no weapons but their hands, their voices and their banners. As a European reporter present at the scene describes: 'This time, the army is there, visibly in position . . . lining all access to the square which itself is occupied by several cordons of soldiers, faceless, gas masks extending from their helmets, rifles aimed, bayonets glistening in the morning sun.'[37]

   8.15 a.m.   A tear gas grenade explodes at the rear of the demonstrators who scatter in confusion into the alleys. But, handkerchiefs over their mouths, they quickly resume their positions, challenging the soldiers, shaking their banners in front of them.

From the military comes a repellent voice, amplified by a loudspeaker: 'This is martial law: you are ordered to disperse; do not force us to shoot.'

The crowd replies: 'We want an Islamic government! Shah is a murderer!'

8.30 a.m.   The tension is mounting. The gathering grows. Cries of joy greet the arrival of Ayatollah Nouri and the demonstrators sit down.

A mass of students and youths sit down facing parliament and, as a gesture of defiance, bare their chests to the guns facing them.[38] Within minutes, several bursts of machine-gun fire interrupt the chants of the protestors. The crowd scatters, screaming. Residents and eye-witnesses assert that after regrouping some youths stand up signalling their readiness for sacrifice and martyrdom.

9.15 a.m.   From the military side comes a cannonade of gunfire as the soldiers in the front ranks open fire at point-blank range without stopping.

There is panic.

It is no contest; it is a massacre. A firing squad at work. Rising out of the eerie silence that follows, the moans and death rattles echo, amplified by the nearby alleys. The square, that one minute before was darkened with people, is now strewn with bodies, shoes, trampled banners, the wounded crawling towards each other. On the side-walks, voices choking with emotion, deeper than before, explode: 'Allah! Allah! See what they have done!' 'They have dared! They have dared!'

Accounts may vary in details, but the indisputable fact is that a wholesale slaughter was ordered. The crime was so horrific that, according to some witnesses, some soldiers refused to fire on the crowd, and, in one famous case, one soldier shot his commanding officer and then himself. This was a deliberate act of terror, to set an example, to create a state of fear and to show the resoluteness of the authorities. The precise number of deaths remains unknown.

According to the foreign press it was up to 500 although some sources estimated the figure to be in the thousands.[39]

The regime's attempt at intimidation backfired as the news of the slaughter enraged rather than frightened the ordinary people of the capital. In southern working-class districts of Tehran a mass demonstration clashed with the army amongst makeshift barricades: 'several of these barricades, defended by youths armed with rocks and molotov cocktails, were destroyed by army units systematically covering the area.'[40] In the shanty towns of southern Tehran, groups of young protestors fought running battles with the troops, disappearing into alleys and side streets when reinforcements were brought in. The sound of machine-gun and heavy artillery fire could be heard almost all day. Eventually, helicopter gunships were sent in to dislodge the rebellious youths and, according to a European journalist, these left a 'carnage of destruction'.[41]

Mass strike

The events of 8 September, known as Black Friday, dramatically changed the dynamic of the revolutionary process. It also left no doubt in the minds of the masses that if they did not destroy the regime it would surely destroy them. Black Friday was the point of no return; the industrial working class now gave their full and active support to the struggle.

The following day, about 700 workers at the Tehran oil refinery struck not, as previously, just for higher wages, but as a protest against the imposition of martial law and the massacre at Jaleh Square. Two days later, on 11 September, the strike had spread to the oil refineries of Isfahan, Abadan, Tabriz and Shiraz. On 12 September, 4,000 print workers and other staff at two leading newspapers in Tehran walked out in protest against the renewal of censorship ordered by General Oveissi, the military governor. On 13 September, cement workers in Tehran went on strike demanding higher wages, freedom for all political prisoners, and the ending of martial law. The wave of strikes hit most towns and cities: cement workers in Behbahan, bus drivers in Kermanshah, workers at the tobacco factory in Gorgan, teachers, bank employees, and even workers in some of the luxury hotels (including, for example, the Tehran Hilton).

By October the strike was no longer confined within individual localities. The dictatorship was being shaken by a tide of strikes as blue- and white-collar workers combined their forces demanding political change. The masses on the streets and the thousands of workers in the factories, offices and services increasingly determined the pace and course of the revolt. However, religion still dominated people's consciousness and the militant clergy commanded almost total allegiance, at least among the crowds on the streets. Early October saw most of the oil fields closed down as well as many refineries. Copper mines at Kerman, the National Bank and some 40 large industrial units were shut by strikes. By the end of October strikes had crippled government offices, telecommunication works, postal services, railways, customs, ports, textile and paper mills, newspapers, universities, schools and bazaars.

The most important strikes in October were those in the oil industry. The oil workers in Khuzistan elected a strike committee to organise the strike and link the struggles of workers in the oil fields, the refineries and the administration. Their political demands, formulated on 29 October, included the abolition of martial law, freedom for political prisoners, and the dissolution of SAVAK. Oil production was completely stopped. At the important oil terminal of Kharg Island, dock workers and other employees had joined the strike, halting all movement of oil off the island.[42]

A number of unsuccessful attempts were made to end the strike and finally the army was used to force the strikers back to work. A founder of the Association of Oil Industry Staff Employees explained:

> They started using methods of intimidation to force us back to
> work. They brought in 200 retired workers and employees,
> paid them enormous sums of money and tried to get them to
> operate the wells. But these people were unable to get the
> installations functioning.
> . . . After this tactic failed, they brought in 200 technicians
> from the navy . . . They got one of the pumping stations
> operating for a while . . .
> The authorities finally realised that we were the only people
> who can operate the oil industry in Iran. And that is why they
> went with troops to the homes of workers in Aghajari and
> Gachsarran [important oil fields] to pull workers out of their

houses and take them to the plants, where they forced them to work . . . This forced labour operation finally raised oil production to four million barrels a day.[43]

The struggle intensifies

The oil strike lasted for 33 days. Meanwhile, demonstrations by other sections of the population spread throughout the country, reaching smaller towns and some villages. As the succession of strikes crippled the economy, riots and bloody clashes continued on the streets, reaching new heights by early November. As one foreign eye witness recalled: 'The sound of gunfire was like an alarm clock waking us up every morning.'[44]

The people had become increasingly fearless despite the overwhelming strength of the army on the streets. In Tehran, between 30 and 60 demonstrators were killed in a clash between students and military units after a statue of the Shah had been pulled down. Angry groups of students and unemployed youths rampaged through the streets shouting 'Death to the Shah'. Banks, luxury hotels, and so on, suffered renewed attacks; buildings, including part of the British Embassy, were burned down.

Ayatollah Khomeini expressed the mood of the masses: 'No gradualism, no waiting . . . We must not lose a day, not a minute. The people demand an immediate revolution. Now or never.'[45] It was clear that the dictatorship had either to crush the uprising mercilessly, using all its military might, or be crushed itself by the rising tide of the oppressed. An American official remarked on 5 November 1978: 'It's completely out of control. The next 24 to 48 hours are critical and could be decisive. The Shah's present government appears to be a lost cause.'[46]

Military government

The Shah replaced Sharif Emami with General Azhari and placed six ministries under high-ranking military officers, after consulting Brzezinski,[47] US National Security Adviser. The appointment of a military government reflected the decision taken by the Shah and his advisers to end the crisis by means of physical intimidation and terror. General Azhari warned that the army would 'remove any obstacle or hindrance' to the restoration of law and order.[48]

The first task of the new government was to get the oil workers back to work and restore production. The minister responsible for labour, General Oveissi, promptly sent the troops into the oil towns of Khuzistan. The army crackdown began on Saturday and Sunday, 11 and 12 November. Hundreds of people were arrested, 30 killed and around 100 injured in the port city of Khorramshahr and at Abadan. By 14 November 'streets were deserted, stores shut, banks ransacked, and cinemas burned. Soldiers, machine guns in hand, guarded the statue of Reza Khan, father of the Shah, and tanks stood at every intersection.'[49]

In fact, from 7 November onwards, the army had moved in every night to arrest workers in their homes and to threaten others. As Paul Balta of *Le Monde* described:

> The soldiers are especially numerous in the working-class quarters of Farahabad and Shahabad – blocks of low yellow-brick houses constructed by NIOC. Tanks, half-tracks, armoured cars, trucks, jeeps with mounted machine guns pointing towards the streets, stand guard threateningly. The military governor, General Esfandiary, announced that he had ordered the arrest of 80 workers considered to be trouble makers. (The workers say there were 140 to 160 arrested.)
>
> Fear reigns in the city. To avoid carnage, most of the 5,000 production workers went back to the refinery. But they work at a slowed-down pace. The other employees (1,500 office workers and 6,000 who run the maintenance services, health care and road repair) have almost all stayed home. The two other factories in the city, belonging to National Petrochemical Company and Nippon Petrochemical, are still on strike, as well as many government offices and municipal services.[50]

The strike was eventually broken, but although the army could force workers to return to their place of work, it could not force them to work. Go-slow tactics were adopted. Thousands of office workers and government employees returned to their desks but refused to work. The oil workers were adamant that they would produce only enough oil for domestic consumption.

There were bitter clashes in Mahabad, Kermanshah and Sanandaj between Kurds and the army. Despite the ruthlessness of the military government and the activities of SAVAK, the arrest of 'trouble makers', more killings and the shut-down of nearly all newspapers, the resistance in the factories, offices and streets never faltered. The struggle continued. The words of a 20-year-old student expressed the feeling of the masses towards the military government: 'It is too late to go back; we have already changed Iran. The army can keep peace for a while, maybe. But in the end the Shah will have to go.'[51]

At the same time the regime tried to appease the mass movement. Five former cabinet ministers, ex-Premier Hoveida, ex-head of SAVAK General Nasiri – in all 132 former officials – were detained. The Resurgence Party was officially dissolved and a commission established to investigate the Pahlavi Foundation. The Shah even went so far as to admit to 'past mistakes':

> I commit myself to make up for past mistakes, to fight corruption and injustices and to form a national government to carry out free elections . . . Your revolutionary message has been heard. I am aware of everything you have given your lives for.[52]

None of these words or deeds fooled the people; on the contrary, it increased their confidence. It proved the fallibility of the mighty Shah and his fear of the mass movement.

The march of the millions

The religiously important month of Muharram began on 2 December with three days of explosive violence and riots. For three consecutive nights, protestors dressed in white shrouds – signifying the will to die – defied the curfew and turned out on the streets. In Tehran, after a call by a radical ayatollah, Taleqani, hundreds of thousands of people spent the night on their rooftops chanting '*Allah-o-Akbar*' ('God is Great'). According to the BBC, some 700 people were killed on the first day alone.[53] In the town of Qazvin about 135 demonstrators were crushed to death by tanks.[54] All over the country similar incidents took place.

On 4 December, the oil workers began a total strike despite repeated threats of dismissal. Sporadic demonstrations and clashes continued in many parts of the country. The tension mounted with the approach of the anniversary of the killing and martyrdom of Imam Hussein (680 AD) – the days of *Tasua* and *Ashura*, the ninth and tenth of Muharram. Strikes spread, street skirmishes increased and the daily clashes resulted in many deaths. The 'rooftop rally' – the tactic of beating the curfew by chanting 'God is Great' from rooftops – became more systematic and widespread. 'After dark', recorded an eye-witness, 'everyone in the city it seemed was out in their garden or on their roof chanting and yelling.'[55] Almost every city and town resounded with the rhythm of incessant chanting during the nightly curfew.

The marches on *Tasua* and *Ashura* (10 and 11 December) confirmed beyond doubt the immense popularity of Khomeini, the hegemony of Islam, and the dominant role of the militant clergy and the mosque. *Tasua* attracted over 500,000 people in Tehran, according to some estimates as many as $1\frac{1}{2}$ million: 'Forty abreast, the marchers converged along various major routes to the Shahyad Monument, built with money extorted from merchants for the 2,500-year celebrations.'[56] The *Ashura* march was even more impressive. In Tehran an estimated 2 million people participated. The march lasted eight hours, with major routes lined with men, women and children, and crowds of people converging from side streets. The lines of people were interspersed by assorted banners in both English and Farsi, reading: 'Hang the American puppet', 'We will destroy Yankee power in Iran' and 'Arms for the people'. In the words of the *Christian Science Monitor*, it was 'a giant wave of humanity' that swept through Tehran 'declaring louder than any bullet or bomb could the clear message: "The Shah must go".'[57]

By 20 December, street clashes between youths – mostly from the shanty towns – and the army, had become a daily affair. As fast as troops with armoured trucks and tanks tore down barricades, others were erected in different streets. Gangs of youths taunted and enticed soldiers into side streets and alleyways only to bombard them with stones and molotov cocktails. A number of police stations were attacked by organised groups.

By the end of December a general strike once again brought the economy to a standstill. Telecommunications, railways and bus services came to a grinding halt; all sectors, from commerce, banking and industry to government offices, customs and ports, had stopped functioning. Strike committees at some of the larger establishments, government departments and communication centres occupied the workplaces. The days of the Pahlavi dictatorship were numbered: 'Once strikes really applied pressure in key areas such as customs, banking and of course the oil fields, their's proved perhaps the most effective weapon to bring the Shah to the realisation that he had to go.'[58]

7. The overthrow of dictatorship

In late December 1978, after unsuccessful negotiations with certain National Front leaders – in particular Dr Sadiqi and Sanjabi – the Shah reached an agreement with Bakhtiyar. On 30 December Bakhtiyar was appointed Prime Minister at the head of a new 'reform' government. Sanjabi and Foruhar were quick to respond and they expelled Bakhtiyar from the National Front. The moderates of the religious opposition under Ayatollah Shariatmadari declared their support for the new Prime Minister as a last hope to halt the move towards civil war and 'anarchy'. Ayatollah Khomeini, however, was uncompromising; he declared the Bakhtiyar government illegal since it had been appointed by the Shah and called for more resistance, strikes and demonstrations.

The stance of Khomeini and the National Front was in accord with the mood of the mass movement. The year 1979 opened with intensified opposition. With the economy at a virtual standstill, hundreds of thousands of people in every major urban centre took to the streets demanding not only the end of the Shah's rule, but also the removal of Bakhtiyar and Khomeini's return from exile. More religious processions, mourning the deaths of December, jammed the streets of the capital and other cities. In the north-eastern holy city of Mashad an estimated half a million people marched on 8 January. The daily street fighting, petrol bomb attacks and bonfires continued unabated, while barricades were built to hamper troop movement.

To calm the situation and perhaps to give the 'reform' government a chance, a Regency Council was named to take the Shah's place while he went on an extended 'vacation'. On 16 January the Shah left the country. Jubilant crowds poured on to the streets; there was a clear sense of victory in the air. But the struggle was not yet over. Bakhtiyar also had to go. Khomeini called for continued demonstrations and resistance to bring down the government. On 19 January more than a million people took to the streets of Tehran, and several million in other towns and cities. Khomeini's decision to return home prompted Bakhtiyar to close the airport, which resulted in a mass protest and the deaths of 28 people on 27–28 January. The airport was eventually reopened under pressure from the movement and, on 1 February, Khomeini returned to Iran to a welcoming crowd of some 3 million people. The final victory of the Islamic revolution was now on the agenda.

The organisations of revolution

The struggle against the Pahlavi dictatorship was, except in the very early phases and during occasional sudden outbursts, well organised. Spontaneous action was quickly harnessed by organisations. However, neither the left nor nationalists could match the influence of the mosque. Islam dominated mass consciousness. The mosque also had the only nationwide organisation which remained, to a large extent, independent of the state and relatively free to operate. No other opposition organisation could muster a network of 180,000 members with 90,000 cadres (*mullas* or low-ranking clergymen), some 50 leaders (ayatollahs), 5,000 'officers' (*hojat al-islams* or middle-ranking clergy), 11,000 theological students (*talaba*, seeker of religious knowledge), and a whole mass of ordinary members such as Islamic teachers, preachers, prayer guides and procession organisers.[1]

Islamic ideology was perpetuated through the mosque's varied and numerous activities in the community at large: the daily prayers within the mosque itself; the *rowze* (sermon); the weekly gathering to discuss religious issues (which cover all everyday activities, behaviour and thoughts); the organisation of pilgrimages, celebrations, ritual feasts (*sofre* attended primarily by women), passion plays, memorial processions, and so on. These organised activities were never totally apolitical, especially during the 1970s. The mosque, therefore, already had a well-entrenched system of thought and activity which was used not only to mobilise and organise the people during the social unrest, but also to manipulate mass consciousness towards its own ultimate political goal.

Throughout the revolutionary process the mosque received funds from the bazaars which it used mainly for political ends.

Strike funds and charitable handouts were distributed to those in need, especially the families of victims of the dictatorship. Increasingly, district and neighbourhood mosques gained control over the daily affairs of their particular area. Even before the overthrow of the Shah they were functioning as local power centres. After the disintegration of the Pahlavi regime they were the natural heirs of political power. Almost immediately numerous local *ad hoc* organisations sprang up throughout the country – the *Komitehs* (committees) of the Islamic Revolution. The vast majority were modelled on mosque organisations and were controlled by the clerical followers of Khomeini.

Among the national minorities and in the outer provinces the committees and popular councils that sprang up were not, on the whole, under the control of Khomeini's men. For example, in Kurdistan the councils (*Shoras*) – formed of members of the Democratic Party of Kurdistan and clerical supporters of Shaykh Ezaddin Husseini (a very radical religious leader) – became the local power centres. In the Baluchi areas, the Arab districts of the south and the Turkoman areas of the north-east, power was generally in the hands of the local intellectuals and clergy who were by no means wholehearted supporters of Khomeini. In Azarbaijan there was a 'hidden' struggle between the supporters of Ayatollah Shariatmadari and followers of Khomeini, which was reflected in the local *Komitehs*.

In the larger urban centres such as Tehran and Isfahan, two main forms of *Komiteh* appeared. The local or neighbourhood *Komitehs* were generally based at the mosque, controlling and organising the particular area under their jurisdiction. Central *Komitehs* also emerged, with far greater powers to co-ordinate, supervise and direct the revolution within the city as a whole – for example, the *Komiteh* of Isfahan established by Ayatollah Khademi. In addition, during the first few months after February 1979, a number of committees were organised by armed volunteers – youths, students and guerrilla sympathisers – whose task was to guard certain streets or areas. Their independence from the mosques and the militant clergy was short-lived.

Thousands of young men were recruited, mostly from the shanty towns, as local armed militia. They became the guardians of the Islamic revolution – the *Pasdaran* or Revolutionary Guards. The *Komitehs* had rapidly become the governing bodies of the main urban centres: they controlled the distribution of food and other necessities and set the prices; they policed the streets, enforcing law and order according to Islamic law (*shari'a*); they combined the administrative and judicial functions of 'government', while the legislative functions rested with the higher authorities of the Islamic Revolutionary Council and Khomeini himself.

Besides these *Komitehs* the revolutionary process had produced other committees based in workplaces, most of which functioned mainly as strike committees. After February many of these committees took over their places of work. Some were forced into this position because the management and owners had fled the country. Others demanded total control or at least, in the case of state-owned enterprises, some form of power-sharing with the owners or managers.

For example, workers at the Chit-e-Jahan textile factory near Tehran elected in February a committee of seven workers:

> A majority of the committee were sympathisers of the *Mojahedin* . . . The elected committee . . . now occupies the former office of the factory's SAVAK agent . . . General assemblies are held once a month, and their purpose is not to delegate decisions but to provide a lecture forum for council members. No constitution or system of recall has so far been worked out, and the original election of the council seems to have had an element of acclamation about it – undoubtedly genuine but no guarantee of democracy in the future.[2]

At the Caterpillar factory, producing construction and agricultural machinery, the committee,

> was composed of 10 manual workers and two office staff. Its political complexion was fairly evenly divided between secular and religious elements – the former including several *Tudeh* sympathisers, and the latter a mixture of progressive and IRP [the Islamic Republican Party, a loose coalition of clerical and militant Islamic groups founded after the 1979 victory] adherents . . . The women workers had been offered a place on the council, but rejected this as tokenism and instead insisted on forming a separate women's council which, among other things, would send an observer to the men's council. The

> council held weekly meetings, and all the members still
> worked at their normal jobs . . . The operation of the factory
> was under the full control of the council, from signing cheques
> and controlling accounts, to determining wage levels. The
> salaries of managerial staff had been reduced and a minimum
> wage established . . . it was clear that the council and the self-
> management of the factory were supported with enthusiasm
> and pride by the workers, whatever their political colouring.[3]

The dictatorship, battered by months of mass demonstrations,
street clashes and crippling strikes, was in a state of near collapse.
Bakhtiyar was fighting a losing battle. Khomeini had already
established his Islamic Revolutionary Council in southern Tehran
and appointed Bazargan as his chosen Prime Minister. The
existence of two irreconcilable governments could not last
long.

The days of insurrection

Although formally the Bakhtiyar government was still in power, in
reality the Pahlavi state machine was no longer functioning as a
state. The army, although still on the streets, was riddled with
dissension. The SAVAK secret police had gone into hiding,
hoping to fight a rearguard action when the time came. The
propaganda mouthpieces of the dictatorship – the state radio,
television, and the official press – although not yet in the hands of
the Islamic revolution were by and large under the control of their
production staffs. Most members of the civil police had disappeared from the streets, awaiting quieter times; some had joined
the revolution.

The dissension in the ranks and desertions from the armed
forces, the principal pillar of the Pahlavi dictatorship, left Bakhtiyar
powerless. In early January 1979 the US administration, with the
full support of its European allies,[4] sent General R. Huyser to Iran.
His mission had three purposes: to ensure that the top ranks of the
disintegrating military establishment remained united behind
Bakhtiyar; to assess the feasibility of a final bid to crush the
revolution, if necessary, by means of a coup; and, if this was not
feasible, to encourage both the military commanders and Bakhtiyar
to reach a compromise with Khomeini in order to keep out the left,

especially the Tudeh Party. The mission was doomed from the start.

Dissension among rank-and-file soldiers, almost entirely conscripts, had begun well before the departure of the Shah. On numerous occasions soldiers had turned their guns on their own officers. In Hamadan in December 1978, for example, a rebel soldier had shot the governor-general. In Dezful another soldier shot his officer; three Imperial Guardsmen in Tehran shot dead 12 officers and injured some 50 men at their Lavizan base. On 30 December, a truck full of soldiers and a colonel joined a demonstration, declaring themselves on the side of the revolution, and, assisted by the crowd, changed into civilian clothing. Many soldiers deserted. Some fled to the villages, others joined the revolution. Many young revolutionaries shaved their heads (a sign of conscription) in order to safeguard the deserters among them.

From autumn 1978 onwards many soldiers refused to fire on demonstrators, and some fraternised openly with them. On 14 January, for example, 'crowds put flowers in the guns of soldiers, soldiers displayed pictures of Khomeini on their vehicles'. After the Shah's departure, 'soldiers and civilians embraced'.[5] Hundreds of soldiers in Mashad and Qom deserted during the month of Muharram.[6] Army officers had to shoot at the crowds (and even at some of their own soldiers) themselves because they could not rely on the rank and file obeying orders.[7]

After one of the daily meetings between US General Huyser and Iran's top generals, it was decided to declare the armed forces 'neutral'. The coup plans seemed to have been shelved, at least for the time being. The military leadership had become increasingly demoralised – by 8 January 1979, General Oveissi and General Mulawi (commander of the Tehran police force) had already left the country – and the army general staff were divided. While some generals were totally opposed to the idea of an Islamic republic, others, more for opportunistic than ideological reasons, had for some time been involved in negotiations with Khomeini's representatives.

Insubordination grew. Many air force personnel, in particular, became increasingly vocal in their support for the mass movement. Some participated in demonstrations openly and in full uniform. Although military sources have denied it, it is alleged that 165 warrant officers were executed for taking part in mass demonstrations. Many were certainly arrested, and a state of emergency had been declared for the armed forces.[8] The royalist commanders were extremely disturbed by this, especially those of the Imperial Guard (with some 20,000 men) and the Immortal Corps (with about 5,000 men) who were trained professionals, hand-picked to protect the royal family. On the evening of Friday 9 February, the Imperial Guard took it upon itself to discipline mutinous air force technicians and cadets (*Homafars*), perhaps hoping to make the rest of the armed forces fall into line. That evening they attacked the Doshan Tappeh airbase in south-east Tehran; the technicians and some pro-Khomeini officers made a stand to defend their base. The news of this attack, viewed by some as an attempted coup, spread swiftly to the rest of southern Tehran. There was an immediate response as large numbers of local youths rushed to the scene. Within a short time, the main guerrilla organisations (the Mojahedin and the Peoples' Fedayeen) had mobilised and raced to the aid of the beseiged airmen, attacking the royalist troops from the rear. It took six hours of intense fighting for the revolutionary forces to drive the Imperial Guards into retreat. The days of insurrection had begun. The rebellious airmen broke into their armoury and distributed rifles, machine guns and other light weapons to the local activists.

As night wore on barricades were thrown up and the whole of south-east Tehran – especially around Jaleh Square – came under the control of armed revolutionaries. Early on Saturday morning truckloads of arms from the air base were moved to Tehran University for distribution. By this time word of the armed struggle had spread throughout Tehran and thousands of volunteers rushed to acquire weapons. During Saturday the guerrilla forces, their armed supporters and thousands of unarmed people attacked nine police stations, some army barracks and the main light weapons factory.

The streets of Tehran had become a battle ground. As Saturday wore on the city was flooded with weapons. Chieftain tanks of the mighty imperial army were showered with petrol bombs as they rumbled through the streets, becoming deadly infernos for their occupants. Ambulances, private cars and trucks filled with armed youths roared through the streets ferrying volunteers to major scenes of conflict.

By Sunday 11 February the fighting had reached its peak, and had overflowed into other cities, such as Tabriz and Isfahan. In Tehran thousands of armed civilians led by the main guerrilla forces stormed the barracks of the Imperial Guard and the Immortals in north-east Tehran and took them captive. Meanwhile, others mounted a successful assault on the military academy and the main army garrison. The Shah's principal residence in Tehran, the Niavaran Palace, was overrun and Imperial Guards on duty forced to surrender. Many local SAVAK secret 'houses' were attacked and captured, revealing torture chambers full of horrifying devices. Evin Prison was seized:

> Using acetylene torches, the attackers cut their way through electrically locked doors to free prisoners at Evin, a jail run by the hated SAVAK secret police. There the liberators found electric whips, torture beds and other interrogation devices that justified many of the atrocity charges long levelled at SAVAK.[9]

The army supreme command abruptly announced its full support for 'the wishes of the people'. The royalists were defeated and the rest of the armed forces either joined the revolution or capitulated. At 6 p.m. on Sunday 11 February, Tehran radio declared: 'This is the voice of Tehran, the voice of true Iran, the voice of the revolution. The dictatorship has come to an end.'[10]

Part three:

Islamic order, reaction and war

8. The triumph of reaction

The ousting of the Shah moved Iranian society into a new phase. It marked the beginning of a period filled with hopes and aspirations for freedom and democracy, but also a period filled with illusion. While the intellectuals and the masses were intoxicated by the spirit of revolutionary action and the joy of victory, the men of God were busy with the mundane task of consolidating their control over society. This phase of the revolution marked the beginning of the breakup of the 'holy alliance' between the secular forces and the mosque.

To complete the Islamic revolution and consolidate its power, the clergy had to suppress or take over the independent workers' committees (the strike committees) and independent local armed units, and ensure that budding grass-roots democracy did not grow. This was not difficult since these committees and units were fragmented and there had never been an attempt to create a nationwide, unified and co-ordinated system of workers' councils.

The collapse of the old dictatorship and the end of its suppression of democratic rights resulted in the blossoming of a multitude of organisations, political parties and associations. There was a flood of books and newspapers; mass meetings and gatherings were held almost everywhere – on the streets, at universities and in offices and factories. The absence of repressive forces on the streets, for a time at least, signalled a period of democracy which was a clear threat to the consolidation of the Islamic revolution.

Within a few months, however, the clergy began a systematic clampdown on democracy in their struggle to establish an Islamic order. The national minorities who had, for the first time in 25 years or so, briefly enjoyed a degree of autonomous political life, and women, were among the first to come under attack. The 'wrath of Allah' was now directed at any popular participation in social, cultural, economic or political affairs not under the control of Allah's representatives on earth. Not only ideological weapons, but also intimidation and physical attacks were used to undermine democracy. The struggle against the clergy, that is the struggle for democracy, was riddled with problems, both ideological and organisational. The dice were heavily weighted in favour of the formation of the Islamic order.

The liquidation of independent workplace committees

Before the revolutionary upheavals of 1978 and 1979 Islamic associations had been established in most urban districts. In 1974, for example, there were 12,300 such associations in Tehran alone.[1] After February 1979 the clergy and the Islamic militants promoted the establishment of Islamic associations in all workplaces – from factories and mines, banks and government departments, to newspapers and the media, as well as in agricultural co-operatives and farms. This was the logical extension of the well-established policy of creating Islamic institutions to facilitate the rule of the clergy.

Khomeini and his supporters were well aware that those workplace (or strike) committees which remained independent of the clergy, especially the workers' committee within the oil industry, were the most important organisations to be taken over by Islamic associations and purged of leftist sympathisers. As *The Economist* reported: 'Aware of the key importance of the strike committee now controlling the oil industry, the ayatollah's minority faction on it has been trying to oust the leftist majority.'[2] Some of these committees were taken over by Khomeini's followers in the early days of February or soon after. For example, the committee at Iran National (a car assembly plant associated with Chrysler UK) was '100 per cent behind Imam Khomeini'.[3] In many cases when the committees appealed to the new regime for financial help, 'this gave the regime perfect justification for sending in its own nominee to take control'.[4]

By August 1979, the workers' committees had been largely taken over by Khomeini supporters, and a year later special government bodies (*Heyat-e Paksazi*) were established to accelerate the removal of dissident workers. Remaining workers' committees which resisted the takeover were finally liquidated by June 1981.[5]

This was only a stepping stone towards the complete regimentation of all workplaces by the Islamic associations. In this they had the backing of special labour groups established by the Islamic Revolutionary Guards Corps, the *Basij* (Mobilisation) organisation and the Organisation of the Mojahedin of Islamic Revolution.[6] These labour groups had branches in the workplaces, especially in the factories, which provided ideological, organisational and military training for hard-line Moslem workers. The primary objective was to establish a monolithic system of work organisation.

The militant followers of Khomeini also promoted Islamic Workers' Councils (*Shoras*), which were to be the institutions of political control of labour at the point of production. Their function in the workplace was identical to that of the *Komitehs* within the community at large. The Islamic councils were never intended to be anything but political institutions, and they must not be confused with the independent workers' committees that sprang up during the revolution. The *Shoras* were, in practice, an extension of the Islamic order within the workplaces. They were, therefore, in no sense 'alternative' organisations of workers' power, nor did they ever initiate genuine workers' control. Indeed, their structure and ideological make-up hindered the self-development of rank-and-file workers. If political and ideological control within the workplace was in the hands of the *Shoras*, direct repression was left to the committees of the Islamic Revolutionary Guards who had established permanent offices in a number of major industries.[7]

The mosque's initial offensive against the left

The clergy recognised that as well as controlling the factories, it was imperative to consolidate their command of the streets. One of the first acts of the new regime was an attempt to disarm the thousands of armed youths acting as independent local militias within the community, especially those connected with the main guerrilla groups. In mid-February Khomeini ordered the revolutionaries to surrender their weapons. He declared that all arms were 'public property' and that their use was 'forbidden by Islamic law' unless permitted by the 'proper authorities'. Identity cards were issued by the *Komitehs* to those acceptable to the local mosque leadership, permitting them to carry arms as members of local militia. However, this attempt was only partially successful because in a number of provinces and outer regions such as Kurdistan and Khuzistan, many people simply refused to hand in their arms.

The only organisations potentially capable of becoming a sizeable force that could challenge the clergy on the streets were the two main guerrilla organisations and the left. They became the principal targets of the clergy's wrath, especially as it became evident that there was growing support for them among the ranks of the armed forces. On Friday 16 February a demonstration of around 50,000 military personnel, in uniform and civilian clothes, protested in Tehran against the composition of the armed forces' new General Staff, and demanded 'a democratic army'. Their list of demands included the complete dissolution of the existing armed forces command structure, the establishment of Revolutionary Committees and the formation of an armed forces' Revolutionary Council elected by the committees. These demands were in line with the platforms of the Fedayeen, the Mojahedin and some other left groups.

Within a few days of this demonstration Khomeini made his first clear move against the left. He banned a planned march by the Fedayeen and announced that the 'organisers are not Moslems and they are at war with the philosophical beliefs of Islam. People of all social strata should not co-operate with them.'[8] The Fedayeen accepted the ban and instead organised a rally at Tehran university which attracted about 150,000 people.

The mosque had its own way of dealing with the left by organising bands of Islamic thugs, called *Hezbollahis* ('members of the Party of Allah'), to attack rallies, meetings and demonstrations not organised by the clergy. The intention was to create an atmosphere of violence and fear in order to halt the development of the left (such as the Fedayeen and other marxist groups) and the radicals (the Mojahedin in particular and other non-marxist groups). Unfortunately the mosque's task was made easy by the inconsistencies and misconceptions of the left itself. The mosque was on the offensive and the popularity of Khomeini was so great that the left and the radicals were either unwilling or incapable of launching their own counter-offensive. Their main weakness was that they lacked experience in mass mobilisation due not only to the years of repression under the Pahlavi regime, but also to their strategy of guerrilla warfare. More importantly, there was no serious attempt to organise a united front against the militant clergy. The divisions (due to ideological differences) among the left and the radicals and their political weaknesses meant that they missed what opportunities there were to mobilise against the mosque. One such opportunity was the struggle for women's rights which came to a head in March 1979.

Women's struggles

A systematic attack on women's rights was one of the most important features of the Islamic regime. Paradoxically, the Islamic revolution had mobilised women on a massive and quite unprecedented scale.

Large, well-organised contingents of women had fought on the streets, not merely supporting the male protestors but acting as dynamic elements of the mass movement in their own right. In the factories, particularly in the textile industry, offices, government departments, schools and colleges, women were among the first to strike against the Shah's regime. In the street skirmishes they provided crucial backup, preparing molotov cocktails, setting up barricades, and so on. There is no doubt that the Islamic revolution to a great extent owed its success to women.

Most observers were surprised not only at the number of women participants but also that the vast majority were veiled. The black *chador*, a veil which enfolds a women's body from head to foot and which was a symbol of women's oppression, had been turned into a symbol of Islamic revolution. During the social upheavals of 1978 and 1979, even women who were against the veil felt obliged to wear it. This was not only to show their solidarity and 'unity' with the mass movement but also to avoid bickering over what was, at the time, considered a 'trivial' matter.

Illusions about unity of purpose with the true victors of the revolution (the clergy) were, for many women, soon dispelled. The first blow came when Khomeini asked the Justice Minister to 'review' the Family Protection Act of 1975, which gave limited protection to women as regards polygamy, divorce and family relations,[9] and ordered him to eliminate all sections contrary to Islamic precepts. This aroused women's anger but only a handful protested. The majority still did not believe that the turbaned 'revolutionary' would betray their rights.

The second blow was struck when Khomeini declared that women working in government departments and agencies must wear the Islamic *hejab*. (*Hejab* is the term for the practice of covering women – the *chador* is the most usual form in Iran.) This time a greater number of women turned their anger into protest and many refused to go to work. Some 10,000 women rallied at Tehran university demonstrating against Khomeini's proclamation. At the same time smaller numbers protested outside government offices.

For almost a week after an International Women's Day demonstration on 8 March 1979, there were meetings and rallies in the capital. The demands included equal pay for equal work, the right to choose what to wear, a greater voice for women in the government, and the preservation of the Family Protection Laws.[10] Thousands of women, mostly unveiled, took to the streets, but they received hardly any active support from men – left, liberal or radical. They were the target of attacks by reactionary Islamic thugs; physically threatened and verbally abused as 'whores' or 'SAVAK and American agents'; some were even stabbed and many beaten to the ground.

This campaign of physical intimidation coincided with well-orchestrated propaganda in support of the *hejab*. This proclaimed the 'dignity' of women under Islam and the necessity of remaining united under Islam against the threat of imperialism. Islamic reactionaries used the involvement of pro-Shah elements in the women's demonstrations to denigrate the women's movement as a whole. Nevertheless, Khomeini called a retreat, declaring that the *chador* was to be 'optional' rather than compulsory. Like a good general, he knew the importance of a timely retreat to prepare for a rearguard offensive.

Within the next few months thousands of women lost their jobs. For example, women TV broadcasters who refused the *hejab* were sacked; women judges were dismissed and barred from practice. Many banks and other institutions began rejecting women applicants. The Family Protection Law was scrapped and a ban on abortion[11] fully implemented. Co-education was banned and young married women were barred from attending schools.[12]

Khomeini's rearguard offensive paid off handsomely. Women

were on the retreat. There was one final attempt by the women's movement to regain the initiative. In Autumn 1979 a number of women's groups attempted to establish a united organisation by convening a Conference of the Unity of Women. This effort was short-lived; not only were women by then relatively isolated but the women's groups were politically fragmented. Most of the groups attending the conference were front organisations for larger political groupings of the far left. They acted within the framework of their parent organisations which invariably saw the struggle of women as important (perhaps for recruiting) rather than as essential. In June 1980 the presidential office of the Islamic republic issued a decree making the wearing of the veil compulsory in all government and public offices. This edict symbolised the defeat of the women's movement and the triumph of reaction.

The main left and radical organisations, including the Mojahedin and the Fedayeen, bear a heavy responsibility for the defeat of the women's movement. The Iranian left paid lip-service to women's rights, but, with the exception of a few small, far-left groupings, it never understood that women have to fight for their own interests as women. It always overlooked the political importance of the struggle against women's oppression, and its vital part in the struggle against Khomeini's reaction. This lack of understanding and practical support became obvious as ever more repressive measures against women were enforced.

The barbaric treatment of women is illustrated by the suffering of women in prison, who may be raped on the basis of Islamic law. A report from Iran explains:

> One family recently received the news of their daughter's execution. The *Pasdars* [Guards] . . . returned her belongings and gave the parents £3, explaining that 'she was a virgin, and since they do not execute virgins in Islam, one of the *pasdars* married her temporarily the night before her execution and the money is the price for the temporary marriage'.[13]

Plebiscite

The campaign to establish an Islamic republic started immediately after the February victory. There was no doubt who was behind the idea: in shops, on the streets, from the south to the north,

Khomeini's portrait and messages were to be seen everywhere. Slogans and tattered banners all over the country proclaimed his 'Imamat' and his 'divine' greatness. As one supporter said: 'We fought for Khomeini . . . and we will fight to keep him. We believe in Allah and Khomeini is Allah's representative on earth.'[14] Could there have been any doubt of Khomeini's landslide victory at the poll?

The plebiscite held at the end of March proved to the world that Khomeini was indeed the true master of Iran. Despite warnings of possible disruption, millions of people went to the polls under the glare of Khomeini's armed guards. The only opposition to the referendum came in the form of abstentions. Many political organisations and groups had criticised the rush into such an important referendum. Some had questioned the meaning of an Islamic republic and its implications, the undemocratic nature of the referendum itself, the bias of the news media, and so on.

However, not all the secular forces abstained. The two main parties that boycotted the referendum were the National Democratic Front (an offshoot of the reformist National Front) and the Fedayeen. The Tudeh Party and the National Front both supported the establishment of the Islamic republic and the Mojahedin took part in the plebiscite reluctantly. The largest number of abstentions was to be found among the regional minorities, especially in the Kurdish, Baluchi, and Turkoman areas where there was a significant boycott and even some fighting at the time of the referendum.

The boycott, although an important gesture of opposition, had no effect on the result of the plebiscite. The vast majority of the urban poor and the rural population had no doubts about Khomeini, who had made it abundantly clear that voting was a 'religious duty' and abstention 'a sin that may open the way to dictatorship'.

Even those organisations which called for a boycott disputed mainly over the form of the referendum. The laying of the institutional foundation of a future theocratic order was hardly challenged. The plebiscite sanctioned Khomeini's Islamic revolution and prepared the ground for the demoralisation and demobilisation of those sections of the anti-Shah movement that were not under the influence of the mosque.

Provisional government

A provisional government was formed in February 1979 and included many members of the National Front and the Liberation Movement. Mehdi Bazargan, one of the founders of the Liberation movement, was nominated by Khomeini as the first Prime Minister of the new regime. However, the provisional government[15] and the militant clergy became increasingly divided. By appointing Bazargan and involving the most prominent nationalist figures, Khomeini had shown himself a capable politician. Although he was no revolutionary, Bazargan was an ideal figure to attract nationalist support. Bazargan was, moreover, a pious and practising Moslem, a religious man well respected by the conservative bazaar. There is little doubt, as Eric Rouleau has observed, that 'the choice of Mr Bazargan as Prime Minister was dictated by tactical considerations at a time when the Imam [Khomeini], recently returned to Iran, feared that the situation could slip from his control.'[16]

The necessity for a provisional government headed by Bazargan was twofold. The Islamic revolution, although powerful at the popular level, had few institutional structures for the full exercise of state power. It needed time to institutionalise the ideological hegemony of Khomeini and to transform the organisations of the revolution into organisations of state power. The provisional government of Bazargan was also intended to demonstrate that only by rejecting even the most rudimentary social demoncracy would Iran be saved. As soon as Bazargan's provisional government had served its purpose and become irrelevant to establishing the Islamic order, Khomeini forced Bazargan to resign on 5 November 1979.[17]

The August crackdown

Before the fall of Bazargan the relationship between secular democratic forces and the mosque had deteriorated greatly. In the first few months after the February victory the new regime sought to undermine grass-root democracy systematically but in such a way as to avoid pushing Iran into a possible civil war. It was not yet capable of launching an all-out assault on its one-time allies, nor did it feel such drastic action was necessary.

One of the new regime's main tasks at this stage was to eliminate or incorporate supporters of the Pahlavi regime and eradicate the threat of royalist counter-revolution. The armed forces were naturally top of the list; many members of the imperial high command, SAVAK agents and royalist officers were executed.[18] A large number of officers suspected of royalist counter-revolutionary tendencies were forced into retirement. A systematic campaign was also waged to incorporate rank-and-file soldiers and the remainder of the officer corps within the Islamic revolution. The militant clergy also created new repressive agencies such as the *Pasdaran*, the Islamic Revolutionary Guards. These were recruited from amongst the most loyal and reactionary elements of the urban poor. Numbering at first about 30,000, the Revolutionary Guards became a parallel force to the national army.

At every stage during these first few months the new regime tested the balance of forces by staging small attacks, such as those on women protesting against the veil, on some newspapers, and on the left. This was not only to gauge the strength of its adversaries, but also to show the incompetence of the secular forces and to prepare the ground among its supporters for a final crackdown.

By August 1979, the militant clergy's efforts to reduce the non-conformist opposition to political apathy were paying dividends. The campaign against democracy had gained tremendous ground among the downtrodden masses, thanks to Khomeini's definition of democracy as defunct, corrupt and satanic, and the simplistic equation of democracy with Western imperialistic exploitation.

In six months the mosque – directed by such high priests of Allah as the Ayatollahs Beheshti and Kani – had tightened its hold on the reins of power through the *Komiteh*, the *Pasdaran*, the Islamic courts and the Islamic Republican Party. The scrapping of the proposed constituent assembly in favour of an Assembly of Experts, which would give final approval to the secretly drafted constitution, was an indication of the regime's growing confidence.

There was no nationally organised resistance to these changes. The peaceful rally called on Sunday 12 August 1979 by the National Democratic Front to demand a constituent assembly could hardly have been anything but a weak gesture of protest. Nonetheless, to show the protestors a taste of what was to come, the *Hezbollahi* thugs were let loose; they broke up the rally, hurled stones at speakers and beat protestors who made no attempt to counter the violence. Placards carried by Khomeini's mob proclaimed: 'Those who want a constituent assembly are counter-revolutionary'.

A week later, the Fedayeen held a rally which attracted about 50,000 people. There were fine speeches by the mothers and fathers of martyred Fedayeen guerrillas, and Khomeini's plan for an 'elected' assembly of 75 expert examiners was criticised as 'unrepresentative of Iran's workers and peasants'. Khomeini's response to these gestures of protest was characteristically uncompromising. He described all those calling for a constituent assembly as being involved in 'a deep conspiracy against the revolution'.

The result of the election to the Assembly of Experts was predictable, with Khomeini's supporters winning comfortably. The turn-out, however, was only about 60 per cent, far lower than in the earlier plebiscite.[19] Although this low turn-out was interpreted as an indication of dissatisfaction with the men of God, what it really showed was the apathy and demoralisation among the discontented sectors of the population – the modern middle class and the intelligentsia.

By mid-August the militant clergy felt secure enough to launch the 'wrath of Allah' to destroy the enemies of Islam, to demonstrate who controlled Iran and to demand total submission. 'The continued strength of the Kurdish movement loomed as a threat to their plans. It was time to put an end to the independent press, to the left, and to the Kurds, each of which, in varying ways, constituted an obstacle to the clergy's project'.[20]

The August crackdown was set in motion by a speech by Khomeini to mark the Day of Jerusalem. He announced that, having allowed the 'conspirators' to show their true faces for the past six months, the wrath of Allah would now smash their conspiracies, break their poisonous and corruptible pens, and stop their attempts to drag the people into 'prostitution in the name of freedom'. He called on the 'Prosecutor of the Revolution' to 'close down all magazines that are against the popular will, and are conspirators; invite all their writers to court and put them on trial'. He also demanded that the leaders of those parties which had engaged in conspiracies be brought to trial and further ordered their members to 'follow the popular path, the path of Islam . . . otherwise they will become the victims of their own wrong-doing.'[21]

The day after Khomeini's speech, Ayatollah Azari Qomi, the Prosecutor of the Islamic Revolutionary Tribunals, proclaimed that the tribunals' jurisdiction had been extended to cover all counter-revolutionary activities. All independent newspapers were declared un-Islamic and banned. Islamic Revolutionary Guards took over the offices of *Ayandegan*, a leading independent newspaper, which had been accused by the Prosecutor-General, Mehdi Hadavi, of drawing aid from the CIA and Mossad,[22] and 12 of its journalists were arrested and faced trial as counter-revolutionaries.

Meanwhile, partisans of Allah armed with clubs, chains, knives and knuckle-dusters, stormed the headquarters of dissident groups, including the Fedayeen. Islamic Revolutionary Guards were ordered to break up all unauthorised demonstrations and it was declared that 'rioters' would face trial in Islamic courts as counter-revolutionaries.

A well-known cleric and patron of the *Hezbollahi* thugs, Hojat al-Islam Ghaffari, addressing a rally of some 30,000 Khomeini supporters, voiced the decision of the militant clergy when he told the crowd: 'We shall stifle any song against Islam . . . We shall not tolerate these opponents of Islam any further.'[23]

The August crackdown also saw the regime's suppression of regional and national minorities intensify, and the formation of the Iranian National Information and Security Organisation (SAVAMA) acknowledged by the provisional government. This was put together by General Fardust from the ruins of SAVAK and was believed to have recruited many former members of the Shah's secret police.

By the end of August the ground had been prepared for the creation of an Islamic theocracy. The clergy's 'revolt against history' had finally crushed the 'holy alliance' and the true victors of the February revolution had dispelled their secular allies once and for all. The turn of the radical Mojahedin and the Islamic liberals was, however, yet to come.

9. Khomeini and the Islamic order

As long ago as 1944 Khomeini had presented a programmatic assertion of the clergy's role in the political structure in his book, *The Discovery of Secrets*. However, at this stage in his political evolution, he had not fully developed his notion of Islamic government which he elaborated in his later book, *The Islamic Government*[1] in 1971. The main theoretical problem for Khomeini was Shi'ite political theory – the theory of *Imamat*.

This orthodox Shi'ite doctrine states, in short, that the Imams were the rightful and legitimate authorities after the death of the Prophet. For the branch of Shi'ism dominant in Iran there were twelve Imams, the last being an absent or hidden Imam (who 'disappeared' mysteriously around 873–4 AD)[2] who would return to govern the Moslem community in the future and establish a 'golden age'.

The Imam, in Shi'ism, derives his authority not from his temporal existence and practice, nor from the community's acceptance of his leadership, but from his *inner*, divinely ordained quality: 'the light of God is within him and it is this that gives him his worldly power and authority.' He is the only person entitled by divine right to govern, that is, to guide the Islamic community towards its unity with God. If the last Imam is absent then, in theory, there can be no legitimate form of absolute authority or government until his return to this world. It follows that devout Shi'ites must remain in opposition until the return of the Twelfth Imam. Moreover, the Islamic state is not a fundamental principle, but only a tool or instrument with which the Imam can remove obstacles on the path of development towards God. The establishment of a state organisation is only authorised, therefore, if necessitated by the movement towards unity with God, in the light of objective conditions.

The essential basis of the theory of *Imamat* is the development of society, the Moslem community, towards unity with God. *Imamat*, the government of the Imam, is not, in orthodox Shi'ism, an end in itself. It is only a means towards the ultimate goal of unity with God. The Prophet himself, it is argued, remained in Mecca for some 13 years inviting people to accept Islam. Only when objective difficulties prevented the Moslem community reaching unity with God did he move towards establishing an Islamic state (in Medina) as a means of overcoming these difficulties. Also, it is argued, when the Prophet died he did not declare a successor because the formation of an Islamic state should not become part of Islamic tradition nor a fundamental principle.

All existing states are, therefore, by definition, illegitimate. They have usurped the authority of God and the Imam and must be opposed and overthrown. The task of the Shi'ite community is to continue its opposition to all forms of state authority and prepare the ground for the return of the 'true' and 'rightful' government of the Imam himself.

Khomeini, while accepting the theory of political opposition within Shi'ite doctrine, claims that the *faqihs* (the Islamic jurists) are the successors of the Prophet until the return of the Twelfth Imam. He argues that state organisation is not solely an 'instrument' to guide the community towards God; it is also to enforce divine authority. Furthermore, he argues that society cannot wait for the return of the Imam, and that the clergy (specifically the *faqihs*) cannot remain in political opposition. It is their duty to put into practice the sacred laws, as would the Imam himself on his return.

Khomeini's theory of Islamic government is, in its essentials, identical to orthodox Sunniism (the main branch of Islam). It is derived from Rashid Reza (1865–1935), the Sunni ideologue of Moslem Brotherhood.

Khomeini, in effect, removed the obstacles within Shi'ite doctrine that had separated the two branches of Islam, and prepared the theoretical ground for the unity of the whole Moslem community.

Khomeini asserts two essential principles of an Islamic order. Firstly, God is the sole legislator and absolute authority. His laws are the laws of Islam and they direct and dictate everything from the most general problems affecting whole societies (and the world itself) to familial relations; from the universal to the particular.[3] Under an Islamic order, therefore, there is no need for new legislation since all necessary laws concerning government administration, taxation, legal and criminal codes, as well as the formation of an army and ministries are already present within the Islamic system of law. He goes on to suggest that the essence and form of these divine laws inescapably lead to the conclusion that they were ordained with the specific purpose of establishing a state structure to administer society.[4]

Khomeini accepts a role for parliament, but not as a legislative body. The purpose of parliament is to establish and clarify policies and programmes according to Islamic law.[5] Parliament must be composed of pious Islamic jurists (*faqihs*), or be under their control.[6] A constituent assembly should also be composed of pious clergy knowledgeable in the laws of God.[7]

Accordingly, Khomeini's second principle of Islamic order is that only those who are learned in Islamic law (the clergy, and specifically the *faqihs*) have real political authority. They inherited from the Prophet and the Imams not only the traditions of divine knowledge, but also the right to govern society.

In the early 1960s, Khomeini set out to create a mass political opposition made up of traditionalist social forces led by the clergy as the guardians of the Shi'ite tradition. By the early 1970s, he had finalised his political theory of direct theocratic rule – nominally, government on behalf of the hidden Imam. Khomeini's movement was no longer to remain in opposition but was intended to become a political force for the realisation of the ideal state, the Islamic theocracy. The mandate of the clergy, according to Khomeini, 'means governing and administering the country and implementing the provisions of the Sacred Law'.[8] Sovereignty belongs to the Islamic jurists (*faqihs*), not to the people. There is no room for democracy in any shape or form; democratic institutions are alien to Khomeini's Islamic order. His determination to establish a theocratic hierarchy did not waiver. His rhetorical allusions to freedom were, unfortunately, misunderstood by many within the anti-Shah opposition, including many on the left. He meant neither freedom for the people nor bourgeois-democratic freedoms. Khomeini was only proposing freedom of Islam – the freedom of the clergy to rule.

Khomeini began to put his ideas into practice from the moment he returned to Iran. An Islamic republic was intended only as a transitory stage towards the ultimate goal of an Islamic theocracy proper. This is why Khomeini was adamant that the proposal for an Islamic democratic republic was unacceptable, even formally.

Islamicisation of society

The judicial structure, which was based on secular law, received immediate attention. The establishment of *Shari'a* (Islamic law) courts was given priority, and clerics swiftly took up duties as 'judge and jury', even before these were assigned to them officially by the Islamic constitution.

Islamic courts began functioning immediately after the February victory and within a short time moved from political to criminal cases. In one week alone during early March 1979, 12 people were summarily tried and put to death for alleged sexual crimes such as prostitution and homosexuality. The *Shari'a* court procedure insists that cases should be almost always completed in a single hearing, with no right of appeal, and that sentences should be carried out within a short time.

In June 1979, while the progressive intelligentsia was engrossed in discussion, its long-cherished dream of an independent judiciary received a final hammering: The Islamic Revolutionary Council published a bill creating special courts to hear a multitude of offences ranging from banditry to strikes. The power and jurisdiction of these courts was so broad that, according to one lawyer, 'an Iranian could be executed for brewing a cup of tea at the wrong time of day'.[9]

The Islamicisation of education and culture, indeed of life in general, was implemented systematically. Music was banned by Khomeini in the summer of 1979 when he declared that music was no different from opium; educational establishments and workplaces were sexually segregated; non-Islamic publications were banned; and a ministry responsible for Islamic guidance was created.

Khomeini the 'saviour'

Islamic ideology played a crucial role both during the revolutionary upheavals and after February 1979, and Khomeini personified the power of Islam. He could summon thousands of people on to the streets and into war against the enemies of Islam. Khomeini became the representative of the masses only to become the fetishised Imam towering above them:

> What has . . . happened is the swift creation of a full-blown cult of personality around the ayatollah. He is proclaimed as 'the Imam'; the crowds strain forward to draw *barak*, spiritual power, by touching him; clothes rubbed against his robes are being treated as sacred relics.[11]

The people's devotion to Khomeini, however, was not based on his Islamic credentials, but on the fact that he was viewed as 'extraordinary' and therefore 'divine'. Indeed, groups of the urban poor were, according to one writer, 'seriously debating whether Khomeini was the Mahdi (Saviour) or merely his precursor. Many would chant: "Three were the idol-breakers – Abraham, Mohammed and Ruholla [Khomeini]".'[12]

Khomeini's anti-imperialism

Integral to Khomeini's Islamic ideology is the struggle against Westernisation: 'All the problems of the East stem from those foreigners from the West, and from America at the moment.'[13] It is also important to see Khomeini's 'anti-imperialist' stance and his 'neither West nor East' principle within the context of the ideological struggle of the clergy. Anything thought to contaminate or corrupt the purity of Islam must originate from an alien source, that is, either from communism (the East) or imperialism (the West). The struggle against these two Satanic forces is therefore the imperative duty of all Moslems, particularly the clergy. This is not essentially a struggle against imperialism (from East or West) but rather a political and ideological struggle against the left and liberals in Iran. It is a focal point for mobilising the masses of urban poor, petty bourgeoisie and other social groups and classes in support of clerical domination and against all those who oppose the rule of the clergy. Khomeini's anti-imperialism, therefore, must not be confused with Iranian nationalism; it is inseparable from his Islamic ideology.

10. Towards an Islamic theocracy

The August crackdown set the stage for the attainment of Khomeini's political ideals, the institutionalisation of clerical power. Together with the militant clergy he set out to finalise the drafting of the Islamic constitution. The Assembly of Experts completed its deliberations on the draft constitution in mid-November. In his inaurgural message to the 'experts', Khomeini reminded them that the 'constitution and other laws in this republic must be based 100 per cent on Islam'.[1]

During September and October, anti-government protests continued occasionally to surface: among women, especially over the new marriage and divorce laws; in Kurdistan; and in the universities. However, the US embassy occupation in November 1979 not only sounded the death knell of the Bazargan government, it also diverted attention from the real problems facing Iranian society.[2]

The US embassy occupation and the Tabriz rebellion

On Sunday, 4 November 1979, some 400 Islamic students, 'followers of the Imam line' (i.e. staunch supporters of Ayatollah Khomeini) occupied the US embassy and seized its diplomats. This was apparently in response to the admission of the ex-Shah to a US hospital on 22 October. Their two main aims were to force the US authorities to extradite the ex-Shah and to maximise public mobilisation in favour of the adoption of the new Islamic constitution. It is doubtful whether Khomeini was aware of the Islamic students' plans to take the American hostages, but he was quick to give his blessing and full support.

Social and economic problems, as well as the all-important struggle of the Kurds for self-determination, had increased markedly by October 1979. Despite the August crackdown, there was growing criticism and protest against the adoption of the draft constitution. The US embassy occupation, therefore, came at a most opportune moment. Khomeini could utilise the real and deeply felt anti-American feelings among the mass of the population to mobilise them under the banner of Islam and 'national unity'. All the problems, especially economic shortages, could be blamed squarely on the Great Satan: the USA.

The mobilisation around the US embassy occupation provided Khomeini with a favourable political climate to silence the critics of the new constitution and to hold a referendum on it. All dissidents were branded either as Zionists or as US imperialist agents. Many political organisations that had previously opposed the constitution now supported it, in order not to jeopardise the anti-imperialist struggle. The referendum itself was not in dispute. Khomeini's backing from the vast army of urban poor and from the majority of the traditional petty bourgeoisie ensured a comfortable majority for the Islamic constitution.

Khomeini's political sagacity in utilising the US embassy occupation can only be fully appreciated in the context of the acute factional struggle that was being waged within the clergy itself. The most important faction among the clergy which had shown reservations about the new constitution was headed by Ayatollah Shariatmadari, whose power lay in his following among the people of Azarbaijan. Shariatmadari had consistently criticised the proposed constitution as an incoherent and self-contradictory legal document and had indicated that he would abstain from voting on it. This would have led to widespread abstentions in Azarbaijan. More importantly, Shariatmadari's continued criticism and opposition could lead, if unchecked, to organised rebellion in Azarbaijan. If this spread to other regions it would threaten the grand project of Khomeini's Islamic theocracy.

A general strike and mass demonstration in support of Shariatmadari were called in Tabriz, the capital of Azarbaijan, on 6 December 1979. The Khomeini faction seems to have taken the initiative in a dangerous but calculated move to force a direct confrontation between followers of Khomeini and of Shariatmadari before the latter could become an organised force. Shariatmadari's home in Qom was attacked and he was the target of an unsuccessful assassination attempt. This precipitated a rebellion in Tabriz in December 1979, which was quashed after a month or so of unrest.

The defeat of the Tabriz rebellion silenced Shariatmadari once and for all. It also meant the downfall of a number of prominent politicians who had supported the rebellion; for example, Hassan Nazih, former director of the National Iranian Oil Company, and Moghadam-Maraghehi, leader of the small Radical Party, were forced, on pain of death, to flee the country. The Moslem People's Republican Party was forced to close down after many of its members had been arrested or executed. Other opposing voices among the high clergy, for example Ayatollahs Shirazi and Qomi, were silenced by the defeat of the rebellion and the US embassy occupation.

The Islamic constitution

The new constitution – which was ratified by a referendum on 2–3 December 1979, did little more than legalise the power of the clergy. What was portrayed as the most revolutionary piece of legislation turned out, in reality, to be the most reactionary. The constitution's introduction makes no bones about its essence: 'The course of affairs is in the hands of those who know God and who are trustworthy in matters having to do with what He permits and forbids.'[3]

Personal liberty, freedom of the press, of association, of assembly, of speech, of religion (with the exception of the Baha'i faith), and similar rights were constitutionally guaranteed, only to be limited by the qualification 'according to Islamic standards'. For example, Principle 26 states: 'The formation of parties, groups, and political and professional associations, as well as Islamic or recognised minority religious associations is free, provided they do not harm the principles of freedom, sovereignty, national unity, *Islamic standards and the foundation of the Islamic Republic*.' (emphasis added). Principle 24 declares the freedom of publication and the press 'unless it is contrary to Islamic precepts'; Principle 27 proclaims the freedom of 'unarmed assemblies and marches . . . provided they do not violate the precepts of Islam'.

Each of the main principles of the constitution contains its own antithesis; it asserts democratic rights and liberties in general terms while denying them with the qualification 'according to Islamic standards'.

But even the most progressive constitutions have provisions, and qualifications that limit the absolute rights of citizens. What makes this constitution uniquely retrogressive are those principles which deal directly with the power structure. The most crucial of these is Principle 5 which gives Khomeini's long-cherished concept of *Velayat-e Faqih* (theologian-jurist regency), a constitutional form. It states that during the absence of the hidden Twelfth Imam, he will be represented by a 'religious jurist' or a 'council of leaders, consisting of religious jurists'. Principle 110 grants the leader or council of leaders such despotic powers that it renders all the remaining principles dealing with the power structure irrelevant. According to Principle 71, the National Assembly is 'authorised to enact laws concerning all issues of a general nature'; yet Principle 72 restricts the authority of the National Assembly to the enactment of laws that do not contradict the 'principles and commandments' of Islam. According to Principle 96, these are determined by a Council of Guardians formed of six selected religious persons and six Moslem lawyers. Who appoints the jurists on the Council of Guardians? According to Principle 110, they are appointed by the leadership – that is, at the moment, Khomeini.

The leadership also appoints the highest judicial authorities, the chief of the general staff, the commander-in-chief of the Islamic Revolutionary Guards, the commanders of the armed forces, and so on. Although Principle 117 states that the President must be elected by an absolute majority of the people, according to Principle 99, it is the Council of Guardians that is responsible for supervising the election, and, according to Principle 110, it is the leadership that must approve 'the competence of candidates for the presidency'. The president can also be dismissed by the leadership.

Only those principles dealing with the relationship between the leadership, the Council of Guardians, the presidency and the National Assembly are absolute and incapable of misinterpretation. The constitution sanctifies the rule of the clergy and secures their domination by entrusting unprecedented powers to the leadership and its appointed Council of Guardians. Together they are the custodians of the Islamic order, the kingdom of Allah on earth. Naturally, in this kingdom, sovereignty belongs not to the people but to Allah (Principle 56) and no law can be enacted which runs counter to the commands of the Koran – the words of Allah. As a result the Koran functions as a sort of alternative constitution, exercising a check on the new Islamic constitution.

Factional power struggles

Once the Islamic constitution had been ratified, the next step was to establish the presidency and parliament. However, the presidential and parliamentary elections of 1980 brought to a head the factional struggle for power. The two most influential contending factions were the so-called religious liberal tendency that found its interests best expressed, at the time, by Bani-Sadr[4] and the fundamentalist tendency represented by the Islamic Republican Party (IRP) under the leadership of the arch-reactionary Ayatollah Beheshti.[5]

The first round in the power struggle went to Bani-Sadr when he achieved a massive victory in the presidential election of 25 January 1980. However, the parliamentary elections of March and May proved to be a triumph for the IRP which gained the majority of the seats. Bani-Sadr received another blow when Khomeini appointed Beheshti as head of the Supreme Court. Indeed, it was becoming obvious that, as far as Khomeini was concerned, Bani-Sadr was expendable. This became clear when Khomeini launched his so-called 'cultural revolution' to rid the Islamic republic of all counter-revolutionaries and Western-orientated liberals.

On 25 April 1980, the US launched a military mission to rescue hostages held in the occupied embassy. Eight helicopters and six C–130 transport planes, carrying an assault team of commandos and support personnel, were dispatched from the aircraft carrier USS *Nimitz* in the Gulf to a site 50 miles south-east of Tehran. The mission failed dismally. Three of the helicopters suffered incapacitating damage and a fourth collided with a C–130 killing eight servicemen. This abortive US rescue mission played right into the hands of the fundamentalists, enhancing their position.

April 1980 also saw renewed attacks by the 'followers of the Imam line' against the last public sanctuaries of the left in the universities. President Bani-Sadr, seeing himself overtaken by events, jumped on the bandwagon and on 18 April gave a three-day ultimatum to all left-wing groups to evacuate their campus offices. In the ensuing days of fierce violence thousands of people were injured, hundreds arrested, several were executed and large quantities of left-wing literature burnt. This was the cultural revolution which aimed to Islamicise the entire educational establishment, and which resulted in the closure of all universities by early summer 1980.

In August 1980 Bani-Sadr received another setback, when the IRP-dominated parliament endorsed Mohammad Ali Rajai as the new Prime Minister, against the wishes of the President.

Meanwhile, the breach between Khomeini and the Mojahedin – which had come into the open in January 1980 when Khomeini refused to approve the Mojahedin leader's candidacy in the presidential elections – had become irreconcilable. Recognising that the Mojahedin were then the most serious potential threat to clerical hegemony, Khomeini intensified his propaganda campaign against them. Calling them 'deviationists' and 'Islamic marxists' in order to discredit them as an Islamic organisation, Khomeini went out of his way not to discourage the violent attacks on the Mojahedin by *Hezbollahi* thugs.

In September 1980 Iraq invaded Iran. This gave Bani-Sadr, as Commander-in-Chief of the armed forces, a short-lived boost. However the lack of success on the military front and the ending of the hostage crisis in January 1981 – after an agreement between the US and Iran was reached in Algiers – proved to be to the disadvantage of the President. IRP-instigated physical attacks on both the Mojahedin and Bani-Sadr supporters continued to increase.

In March 1981 a rally sponsored by Bani-Sadr to commemorate the death of Mossadeq was attacked by a *Hezbollahi* mob and the President ordered his supporters to counter-attack. The IRP immediately accused the President of 'incitement to riot' and IRP MPs called for him to be prosecuted. By June 1981 it had become clear that Khomeini had turned against Bani-Sadr: 'Listen,' he warned the President, without naming him, 'I shall do the same [to you] that I did with the Shah.'[6] Repent or be crushed was his message and he dismissed Bani-Sadr as Commander-in-Chief.

A few days later Bani-Sadr was forced to go underground as *Hezbollahi* thugs, IRP members and their supporters called for his execution. With the fall of Bani-Sadr and his escape (with Masud Rajavi, leader of the Mojahedin) to France, the Islamic republic entered a period marked by the complete ascendancy of the clergy.

However, the struggle for control of state power was far from over. Intense factional differences continued to plague the Islamic regime. Today there are two broad tendencies locked in struggle for power: the followers of the 'Imam line'; and various groups and individuals opposed to it who can be labelled as the 'traditionalist–technocratic' tendency. It must be emphasised that this second tendency is much broader than either 'traditionalists' or Islamic 'technocrats'. For example, it includes former premier Bazargan and his religious liberal followers, and the *Hojatiyeh* group of ultra-reactionary clerics (formed in the 1950s as an anti-leftist and anti-Baha'i group with some connections with SAVAK). It goes without saying that both tendencies are reactionary and both are firmly committed to the preservation of the Islamic republic. The differences between them arise over who controls the regime and how best to preserve and strengthen its hold on society.

The Imam line

This tendency, besides having a majority in parliament, also influences a number of organisations that came into being as a result of the Islamic revolution. These include, for example, the Islamic Revolutionary Guards, the Islamic *Komitehs*, Islamic Associations, the *Basij* (Mobilisation) Organisation, the Economic Mobilisation (*Basij*) Organisation, the *Mostazafin* (Disinherited) Foundation and the Organisation for Islamic Propaganda. It also embraces the Tudeh Party and the Fedayeen guerrilla organisation (majority faction).

The traditionalist–technocratic

This tendency is influential in the government itself and in such bodies as the Council of Guardians, the Supreme Council of Justice, the Supreme Defence Council, the Supreme Economic Council and the Supreme Council of Propaganda.

The traditionalist–technocratic tendency accuses the Imam line of pursuing ruinous economic policies such as:
—appropriation and redistribution of wealth and property;
—state monopoly of foreign trade;
—extending the nationalisation of industry and halting attempts to privatise already nationalised industries;
—giving full control of commodity distribution to *Komitehs* and the Economic Mobilisation (*Basij*) Organisation;

—radical economic reforms in the interests of small companies
   and medium-to-small merchant ventures;
—state involvement in production and distribution;
—the strengthening of the Islamic Councils (*Shoras*) in workplaces.

It also argues that certain of the Imam line's policies have turned
a large number of people, in particular the middle classes, against
the Islamic republic and if continued could threaten the very
survival of the regime. Such policies include the exercise of law
enforcement by the *Komiteh*s and Islamic Revolutionary Guards
without recourse to the Public Prosecutor's Office; the independence of the Islamic Revolutionary Courts from the Ministry of
Justice, and the resultant arbitrary activities of these bodies.

The traditionalist–technocratic tendency is accused by the
Imam line of following quite the opposite economic policies;
supporting privatisation, the big merchants of the bazaar and
large companies, worshipping private property, and promoting
government control over all affairs.

There are some strategic differences between the two tendencies:
the Imam line supports state control of the economy although
various factions within the tendency support it to different
degrees; while the traditionalist–technocratic tendency supports a
mixed economy – 'private' capitalism with overall state super-
vision.

However, there is no difference between the two tendencies as
far as centralisation of power is concerned. If the Imam line tends
to argue for the independence of bodies such as the *Komitehs*, the
Islamic Revolutionary Guards and the Economic *Basij*, it is simply
because it is well aware that their incorporation within ministries
and government departments would mean that control over them
would go to the traditionalist–technocratic tendency. The conflict
is over the overall control of power. The traditionalist–technocratic
tendency, for example, is not necessarily opposed to the existence
of *Komiteh*s or Islamic Revolutionary Guards. Nor is the Imam
line in principle against government control over such organisations. These are tactical rather than strategic issues.

Khomeini's role has been decisive in holding the balance
between the two and preventing an all-out confrontation (although
there have been violent clashes). What does seem certain is that

Khomeini's death would sooner or later unleash a final showdown between the two tendencies.[7] If, as a result of this, the armed forces were brought into play (most likely on the side of the traditionalist–technocratics) then Iran might face a bloody civil war.

11. The fight against reaction

The ousting of Bani-Sadr was the last straw that forced the opposition to Khomeini's regime to turn to armed struggle.[1]

On 20 June 1981, countrywide urban guerrilla warfare began with street demonstrations by various anti-Khomeini groups, prominent among them the Mojahedin. Violent clashes followed with the forces of reaction – the Islamic Revolutionary Guards and the *Hezhollahi* thugs. Hundreds of protestors were arrested, many executed on the spot, and many of the injured were left bleeding on the streets.

On the morning of 28 June, while Ayatollah Beheshti was addressing the leadership of the IRP, an explosion killed 72 of them, including Beheshti himself. This decimation of the IRP leadership, especially Beheshti's death, was a severe blow to the organisation.[2] The Islamic authorities reacted swiftly. Literally thousands of Mojahedin supporters and left-wingers were summarily executed on the streets and in jails and many more were imprisoned. Some were aged only 13 and 14. The Tehran prosecutor had asserted that, 'on the basis of Islam a nine-year-old girl is considered mature. So there is no difference for us between a nine-year-old girl and a 40-year-old man, and it does not prohibit us from issuing any kind of sentence.'[3]

On 30 August a second explosion blasted the office of the Prime Minister, killing the new President of the Islamic republic, Rajai, and his Prime Minister, Bahonar. Retribution was rapid. Within a day, some 40 people were reported to have been executed, 23 Mojahedin and the rest supporters of various left-wing groups. During one weekend at the end of September 1981, Khomeini's vengeance took the lives of 128 men and women in Tehran and four provincial towns alone.[4] Their crime was 'war against God', an offence covering a whole range of political activity from distributing leaflets to attacking the forces of Islamic terror.

The clergy showed no remorse or mercy. The Prosecutor-General, Hojat al-Islam Tabrizi, declared in autumn 1981 that in future the Islamic Revolutionary Guards should arrest fewer rebels in order to save the expense of their internment. Instead, he proclaimed, there should be 'street trials at which the testimony of just two *Pasdars* will be sufficient for death sentences to be carried out on the spot.' The Chief Islamic Judge of Tehran, Ayatollah Guilani, also asserted, in the name of Islam, that injured rebels should be 'finished off' where they lay.[5] Khomeini himself legitimised such butchery by invoking the traditions of the First Shi'ite Imam: 'The glorious Imam,' he stated, 'killed in one day 4,000 of his enemies to protect the faith.'[6]

In spite of the reign of terror that followed the two explosions, there were scores of clashes between left-wing and Mojahedin guerrillas on the one side, and the 'soldiers of God' on the other. Each guerrilla attack on the authorities resulted in more arrests, still more executions and greater repression. Despite extensive guerrilla operations and armed resistance, the regime has contained the underground resistance, seriously weakening it by murdering some of the Mojahedin's leaders[7] and decimating some of the smaller left-wing organisations, for example, the Maoist *Peykar* and the Minority faction of the Fedayeen.

The major problem faced by the underground movement is the demoralisation of the opposition since the August 1979 crackdown. Although the Mojahedin, as the most powerful opposition force in Iran, undoubtedly enjoys substantial support, it has proved unable to mobilise and involve a sizeable section of the population in the struggle against Khomeini. This indicates the ineffectiveness of a guerrilla strategy, on its own, to transform indirect support from sections of the population into direct action to overthrow the regime. The assassinations and hit-and-run tactics of the Mojahedin have merely hurt the regime. Moreover, the regime has become far more brutal in its response to the opposition. Indeed, since its formation, the Islamic republic has transformed itself from a repressive regime into a liquidationist state. Since September 1981, the regime has tried to liquidate all opposition elements in the factories and other workplaces.[8]

In 1983, according to some estimates, there are over 50,000 political prisoners in Iran. The use of torture has become systematic, and dozens of 'counter-revolutionaries', mostly in their teens, are executed every week. A former prisoner states: 'Night and day you can hear the sound of gunfire in Evin [the main prison and torture centre in Tehran].'[9] The active opposition movement in Iran paid a heavy price for its armed resistance, with something in the region of 12,000–20,000 opponents of the regime killed between mid-1981 and mid-1982.[10]

The struggle against the regime continues, however, despite the reign of terror. The opposition to the Khomeini regime is organised mainly from outside Iran itself. It involves a range of groups and individuals from the monarchist followers of the new 'Shah' and right-wing forces such as those of Bakhtiyar, to radical centrist democratic currents like the National Democratic Front (NDF) and small revolutionary left groups such as the Union of Communists, Fedayeen organisation (Minority faction) and *Paykar* (a Maoist group). The most important oppositional force remains the Mojahedin and their National Council of Resistance (NCR) which it sponsors. The NCR includes a number of important political parties, such as the Democratic Party of Kurdistan, the NDF, followers of Bani-Sadr (who is 'provisional' President) and some of the most influential left-wing and secular democratic (nationalist) intellectuals. Its principal objective is to replace the Islamic republic with a Democratic Islamic republic. It is a popular front grouping fully controlled by the Mojahedin. In spite of a number of demands which sound progressive – on women's rights, democracy, the national and ethnic minorities – the dominance of Islamic ideology makes these extremely suspect. For this and other reasons most of the revolutionary left groups, whose divisions make them unlikely candidates as an alternative force, have refused to join the NCR.

The Mojahedin have a substantial base among students, sections of the petty bourgeoisie and the working class, and according to some estimates have at least 30,000–40,000 cadres and perhaps as many as one million supporters inside Iran. Given their organisation and their Islamic ideology and programme, at the moment they are the only current that may have some chance as an alternative to the present regime. But for the same reasons, and because of their elitism, if successful the Mojahedin could easily be a repressive force pushing Iran towards a fully regimented society.

12. Economic chaos: between crisis and collapse

That the Islamic regime is in serious economic trouble can hardly be disputed. The Iranian economy had stagnated during the last few years of the Pahlavi regime and the problems were compounded by the upheavals of the Islamic revolution. Far-reaching solutions were required. However, divisions in the Islamic movement have prevented even a cursory programme of economic reforms. From its foundation the Islamic republic was haunted by the spirit of Islamic tradition and Koranic principles on economic matters. The interpretation and practical application of this tradition and these principles were widely disputed. However, from the most radical interpretation of Islam – that of the Mojahedin – to the most reactionary – that of Khomeini himself – a fundamental transformation of the economic structure of Iranian society has never been at issue.

All the important economic measures that were taken, from the Bazargan government onwards, were essential to stave off the complete collapse of the economy. The apparent emphasis on 'economic nationalism' and autarky was less the application of an economic strategy than a desperate response forced by the circumstances of the day. The exodus of the old capitalist magnates before and after the February victory forced the government to nationalise many industrial enterprises as well as the banking and insurance sectors. Neither Bazargan nor Bani-Sadr were able to implement their own economic programmes because of the political chaos and because of the divisions within the regime itself. Since the departure of Bani-Sadr, the internal rift has aggravated economic confusion by preventing the emergence of any coherent economic strategy. What measures have been implemented have been insufficient to check the economic slide.

During the regime's first year Iran's industrial production declined considerably. Most enterprises operated at only half capacity and some stopped completely. It has been estimated that the Gross Domestic Product fell from \$492bn in 1978 to \$406bn in 1979, a drop of 17.5 per cent.[1] Many of those enterprises still producing laid off a large part of their workforce.[2]

Deprived of capital, foreign loans, spare parts (as a consequence of the Western economic embargo) and technical and managerial staff, the level of output declined even further during 1980. By the first half of 1982 most factories were still functioning at only a fraction of capacity.[3] In addition, many of the previous regime's industrial projects were cancelled.

One of the most important economic aims of the Islamic revolution, according to Bani-Sadr and Khomeini himself, was to improve agricultural production to achieve self-sufficiency. Yet according to the US Department of Agriculture, the cost of food imports to Iran rose from \$2.8bn in 1980 to \$3bn in 1981, and would have reached \$4.5bn to \$5bn in 1982.[4]

The regime's agricultural policy has been, to say the least, extremely confused. At first it encouraged small-scale farming and migration back to the land from the cities. Later, it attempted to push through a system of land division based on a countrywide limit of 20 hectares per farming household.[5] The failure of this policy led to its being abandoned and the regime's policies became little different from those of the Shah. One of the major problems – besides the lack of capital investment and shortages of fertilisers and other agricultural inputs – is the indecision over private versus state ownership of land; meanwhile agricultural production continues to decline.

The expectations and aspirations of large sections of the population for better economic conditions remain unfulfilled. The standard of living for most people has, in fact, fallen drastically since the revolution. Although the precise number of unemployed is not known, estimates put the figure at 2–4 million, out of an economically active population of 11.5 million.[6] Only 800,000 of the unemployed receive a subsistence allowance.[7] The rest have either to rely on family and friends or to fend for themselves; many have become involved in petty trading and street peddling which has increased enormously.[8]

Central to the deterioration of Iran's economy has been the drop in oil revenue, both as a direct result of the war with Iraq and also, despite claims to the contrary, because of managerial and internal social problems. Shortages of spare parts in the oil industry, although an important problem earlier on have, apparently, been largely overcome through increased domestic manufacture.[9] The major problem, however, is the difficulty of finding markets for oil, given the effects of the world economic recession.[10] A further factor which has reduced oil revenue is inflation and the unfavourable exchange rate between the US dollar and the Iranian rial. The regime's oil revenue in 1983 is worth only a fraction of what it was in 1978.

Estimates for the annual rate of domestic inflation vary between 25 per cent (based on official Central Bank figures) and 85 per cent.[11] Whatever the actual figure, there is no doubt that prices, and particularly those of food, have soared. Food prices on the black market increased, according to one estimate, by at least 400 per cent between 1978 and late 1982.[12] Meat, for example, which is rationed to 100 grams per person per week, costs on average £2.50 (350–450 rials) per kilo. On the black market the price is £7 (1,200 rials). Rationed petrol is 20p a litre, on the black market it is 80p.[13] According to Eric Rouleau, rents, which had dropped sharply after the fall of the Pahlavi regime, increased again by 1980 to the extremely high levels of 1977–78,[14] and have stayed high ever since.

Most basic foods and goods are rationed, but an inefficient and corrupt distribution system has caused much hardship, with long queues forming as early as 4 a.m. A recent report from Iran states:

> A wide layer of people now make their living dealing on the black market, buying and selling coupons. All of this requires the closest involvement of the bureaucracy and the top officials. Among the biggest centres of such corruption are the state-run co-operatives for officials where food and other goods are more readily and cheaply available than elsewhere. Up and down the apparatus the commission agents are at work. They take their percentage, as high as 20 per cent on each deal. Premier Moosavi, and Rafsanjani [Speaker of Parliament], to name but two, are involved in the corrupt selling of both oil and foodstuffs.[15]

All the evidence points to an accelerated economic decline, especially given the immense drain on resources of the Iran–Iraq war. Lack of confidence in the regime and uncertainty over its economic policies has meant little or no private capital investment and the difficulties facing the state preclude any significant public investment, at least in the near future. Future economic prospects seem bleak.

The working class, state employees and salaried professionals have borne the brunt of this rapid economic decline. Cutbacks in public spending, factory closures, large-scale lay-offs and part-time working, mean not only hardship for the working class but also a significant reduction in their industrial power. Strikes, which have occurred both in the oil industry[16] and in other industries such as steel,[17] have far less impact than previously. While it is true that workers are still a relatively powerful class economically, their power is hardly comparable to what it was during the last years of the Pahlavi regime.

Despite immeasurable hardship, the economic crisis has not resulted in any significant *mass* political unrest. One reason for this is the absence of political work by the oppsition in the working class and among the unemployed; another is the climate of fear. There is a further important reason: the support given by Khomeini to sections of the uprooted migrant peasantry, the lumpen proletariat, as well as to the traditional petty bourgeoisie. Since his victory Khomeini has consistently portrayed himself as a champion of the 'disinherited' – the urban poor, augmented by the displaced residents of the war-stricken provinces. He appears as their patriarchal benefactor, with the *Shahid* (Martyr) Foundation, Imam's Relief Committee and the *Mostazafin* (Disinherited) Foundation organising relief work among this section of the population. The state subsidises essential food stuffs, paid for mostly by the cut-price sale of oil[18] as well as by reductions in 'development' projects and in wages and salaries.

It is, therefore, still oil revenue that has saved the regime on the economic front,[19] although the depletion of Iran's overseas assets has also helped. A budget deficit of $11.4bn in 1980–81 was largely offset, for example, by the reduction of Iran's foreign exchange reserves by about $8bn.[20] In early 1981 Iran's foreign assets stood at only $4bn, including $2bn transferred after the ending of the hostage crisis. Foreign currency reserves in November 1981 were estimated at no more than $2bn, and, according to the exiled Central Bank Governor Ali Nobari, they stood at only $600 million.[21]

As long as the regime can produce and sell oil, it can maintain itself and keep the economy from collapse. But before a viable economic programme can be implemented, internal and regional order has to be restored.

13. The struggle of national minorities

From its foundation the Islamic regime has been haunted by the spectre of regional disintegration. Khomeini's Islamic theocracy entails a monolithic political system; indeed the centralisation of power is inherent in Islam – the total submission to a single authority (Allah). Yet Iran is made up of various national and ethnic minorities – Kurds, Arabs, Baluchis, Turkomans, and Azarbaijanis, numbering some 20 million people – most of whom have shown varying degrees of reluctance to be incorporated into Khomeini's Islamic monolith. The regime's attempts to unify the country under the rule of the clergy and the banner of Islam have been met by waves of social unrest and, in a number of regions, armed resistance.

Kurdistan: bastion of resistance

As early as mid-February 1979, armed youth in the Kurdish town of Sanandaj captured the new government's city police chief, Ali Jamshidi, and the situation throughout Kurdistan became extremely tense. According to the state radio, 'anti-revolutionary elements' in Kurdistan were planning to march on military barracks in the towns of Saqez, Baneh and Marivan. On 23 February, a mass demonstration in Saqez was held, demanding autonomy with the marchers chanting, 'Independence for Iran, Autonomy for Kurdistan'.

The provisional government's response to the Kurdish demand for autonomy was mixed; on the one hand the then Labour and Social Affairs Minister, Dariush Foruhar, was asked to examine the Kurdish issue; on the other, it vowed to crush those provoking unrest. Khomeini, however, was adamant and demanded that all political parties in the country (a reference to Kurdish organisations) must work within the framework of Islam.

The Kurds were unyielding. As Shiekh Ezzedin Husseini (one of the most outspoken radical leaders of the Kurdish nationalist movement) stated in March 1979, 'If we cannot solve it [the question of national autonomy] by peaceful means, we will find some other ways to solve the question.'[1] The Kurds had *de facto* control in many towns and villages. Mahabad was under the control of the Kurdish Revolutionary Committee, independent of Khomeini's supporters. Kurdish militias controlled many army barracks and guerrillas were well-entrenched in the mountains ready to defend their rights.

All the significant political organisations and influential figures in Kurdistan – the Kurdish Democratic Party (KDP) headed by Abdolrahman Qasemlou, the Toilers' Revolutionary Organisation of Kurdistan (Komala), and Ezzedin Husseini – agreed on one basic issue: self-determination does not mean secession, separatism or independence from Iran, but autonomy. This is explained as the right to have a Kurdish administrative system; to have Kurdish as the first language of the region; and to have internal security in the hands of the Kurdish authorities. Apart from foreign relations, defence, and long-term economic planning, they demand control over all other matters by a Kurdish regional government. They insist that the question of autonomy has nothing to do with religion, with the fact that they are Sunni Moslems rather than Shi'ites.

These demands were put to Khomeini early in 1979, but they fell on deaf ears. In March fighting broke out between Kurdish rebels and Iranian forces, when Kurds called on the army garrison in Sanandaj to hand over weapons and ammunitions. After the army's refusal Kurdish rebels besieged the garrison, took over the radio station, police and gendarmerie headquarters. The guerrillas established their own revolutionary committee to run the town in opposition to the pro-Khomeini *Komiteh*. After three days the central government managed to halt the heavy fighting with the promise of a plan for self-rule. The plan was aimed at cooling the situation and preventing the spread of Sanandaj rebellion.

Between March and August 1979, while the major left-wing organisations in Iran were engrossed in internal discussions, the Kurdish nationalists were busy organising for the inevitable showdown with the Islamic regime. In August 1979 the regime felt strong enough both to attack the left and also to order the army and the Islamic Revolutionary Guards to enter Kurdish towns and villages to restore order. Khomeini had, in effect, declared a 'holy war' on the Kurds; he was particularly concerned about the growth of the KDP which had become the most influential and best organised force in Kurdistan.

However, although the August crackdown was generally successful against the left in Iran, the campaign against the Kurds was a failure. The army, which had little inclination for this war, and the *Pasdaran*, suffered heavily at the hands of the Kurdish *Peshmergas* (guerrillas). Again there were attempts at reconciliation with religious liberals and the progressive clergy acting as mediators.[2]

Neither Khomeini nor the IRP were willing to compromise their stance on the issue of autonomy. As late as December 1979, the KDP leader, Qasemlou, was allowing the possibility of compromise with the regime. As he put it in an interview with *Le Monde*: 'Whatever the character of the regime, it is less its ideology than the relations of force that will decide the outcome of the conflict. This is why I do not exclude a compromise acceptable to the Kurdish people.'[3]

It was certainly the 'relations of force' that were decisive, turning Kurdistan into a land of resistance. In March 1980 the regime resumed its war against the Kurdish people. By September, when the war with Iraq had begun, there were as many as four divisions involved on the Kurdish front. This was in addition to some 40,000 Islamic Revolutionary Guards, who were committing atrocities against the Kurdish people. Mahabad, the citadel of Kurdish nationalism, was repeatedly bombed by the air force.

The *Peshmergas* had already begun to evacuate the major towns, to avoid a wholesale massacre of Kurdish citizens and to carry on the struggle in the mountainous terrain where they are almost invincible. The Kurdish resistance front controls more than 60,000 square kilometres of the region.[4]

Kurdistan has become a bastion of democratic forces; the KDP was one of the first organisations that joined the National Council of Resistance.[5] Khomeini's regime has so far failed to defeat the Kurds, even though it has deployed about 45,000 regular Iranian troops in addition to the *Pasdaran*, against 12,000 *Peshmergas* and 20,000 armed villagers.

Crushed rebellions

Unfortunately for the Kurdish nationalist movement, and for the Iranian left in general, during the first year of its life the Islamic regime was able to defeat the rebellions of other national and ethnic minorities. For a while, however, during the first months of 1979 it seemed that the Islamic republic was encircled by rebellious nationalist forces from the Turkomans in the north to the Baluchis and Arabs in the south.

Some Baluchi intellectuals, clergy and local businessmen, organised a clandestine political organisation, the Islamic Unity Party (IUP), to champion the cause of Baluchi nationalism. The people of Baluchistan live in an economically and socially depressed and backward region. Neglected and suppressed they exist in what can best be described as an arrested condition between tribalism and nationhood. Nevertheless, their aspiration to see Pakistani and Iranian Baluchistan unified is not to be taken lightly. Although the IUP demands autonomy, there are more radical and left-wing elements who go much further, calling for an independent united Baluchistan. The struggle of the Baluchis, unlike that of the Kurds, as yet represents only a potential threat to the Islamic regime. However, if organised and united with their compatriots in Pakistan, they could pose a threat not only to Khomeini's regime but also to Zia ul-Haq's dictatorship.[6]

In late March, Turkoman rebels in the north challenged the Islamic authorities by capturing both the police and gendarmerie headquarters, effectively taking control of the town of Gonbad-e Qabus near the border with the USSR.[7] The High Council for Turkoman Homelands produced a list of political and economic demands, the two basic issues being autonomy and the return of Turkoman lands. Within a matter of days the Iranian armed forces, backed by a large contingent of Islamic militants, retook the town after fierce fighting. The battle of Gonbad lasted some 10 days and about 400 Turkomans were killed.[8] However, this defeat has not brought to an end the issue of a Turkoman homeland.

It was not long before the regime was once more challenged in the south-west. This time, however, it was in the land of 'black gold' and the threat was to Khomeini's finances. The oil-rich region erupted in late spring 1979. The port town of Khorramshahr was shaken by heavy fighting between Arab nationalists and army units backed by navy gunboats, commandos, Islamic Revolutionary Guards and *Komiteh* gunmen, who were ordered by the Governor-General, Admiral Madani, to crush all Arab resistance.[9] During two months of unrest many activists were arrested, tried by Islamic Revolutionary Courts and executed for the crime of waging 'war against God'. The area then remained superficially quiet until it became a battle zone in the war with Iraq. However, the killings of Arab nationalists have undoubtedly left a mark. As an old Arab woman put it, 'We thought Khomeini would give us water and schools. But, instead, he [sent] men to kill.'[10]

In December 1979, Khomeini's troops were once again on the march, this time to quell an insurrection in Tabriz, capital of Azarbaijan. This uprising was not a struggle for autonomy, however, but a showdown between the supporters of Ayatollah Shariatmadari and those of Khomeini. Although Azarbaijan has a long history of struggle for self-rule, the Tabriz insurrectionists were fighting for the repeal of the newly ratified constitution, out of loyalty to Ayatollah Shariatmadari. It was a significant move by the Azarbaijanis and, had it been supported, it could perhaps have spread. However, none of the major political parties – including the KDP, the Fedayeen (who after initial support reversed their stance) and the Mojahedin – took a single step to support the insurrection. It was crushed by a ruthless pro-Khomeini counter-offensive. The Azarbaijanis, largest of the ethnic minorities, have since remained silent.

The struggle in Iran is such that the national minorities, in their battles for self-determination, undermine the Islamic order although they are powerless as an independent factor in the struggle against the regime. The right to self-determination is therefore not merely an abstract 'principle' but a force of revolution.

14. The Iraq–Iran war

Contrary to the declarations of Iranian nationalists and the rhetoric of Islamic reactionaries, the Gulf war cannot be regarded simply as an act of aggression on the part of Iraq. That Iraq did invade Iranian territory is not disputed. However, it is crucial to see this aggression as only one event in the historical relationship between the two countries. The Gulf war is inseparably linked to the political conditions in both Iran and Iraq. Clausewitz' maxim that war is a continuation of politics by other means is precisely the case here. Therefore, the question as to which of the two reactionary regimes first drew the gun has little significance.

From politics to war

In February 1979 the relationship between Iran and Iraq was formally cordial. Within a matter of months their relations had deteriorated sharply. The main reason for this was that Iraq's Ba'athist regime was becoming increasingly concerned about internal security and the threat of an Islamic revolution assisted by Iran.

Khomeini and many of his militant followers had consistently proclaimed their ambition of spreading the Islamic revolution. Soon after the establishment of the republic the Iranian clergy stepped up its propaganda campaign, inciting the Shi'ite communities of the Gulf states to rebel against their corrupt ruling regimes. It also began to actively support various Shi'ite opposition groups.

The Iraqi regime felt more vulnerable than other Arab states in the Gulf region, given that over 55 per cent of its population of some 13½ million were Shi'ites, a large majority of whom had suffered under the regime and were impoverished second-class citizens. Moreover, any threat of revolution has to be taken seriously by a regime which governs only by the consent of a minority ruling bureaucratic class and relies heavily on repression.

Soon after Khomeini's victory the Ba'athist Iraqi dictatorship, headed by President Saddam Hussein, began its own programme of propaganda and agitation against the new Islamic regime. By the middle of 1979, both sides were involved in plots and counter-plots against each other.

The Iraqi opposition, whether inspired by the Khomeini regime or actually organised by it,[1] became increasingly dangerous. There were more and larger demonstrations, assassinations, and attacks on Ba'athist party offices, police stations and units of the People's Militia. The violence claimed some prominent victims, among them Barzan Takriti, Saddam's brother, right-hand man, and supreme chief of security. There were also two or three attempts on the life of Vice-Premier Tariq Aziz. Large numbers of Shi'ite oppositionists were arrested and some tens of thousands were thrown out of Iraq. The Da'wa party – the Shi'ite opposition party – was outlawed and all its members threatened with immediate execution. In April 1980, Saddam's regime summarily executed a religious leader of the Iraqi Shi'ites, Baqir Sadr, and his sister – committing, in the eyes of Khomeini, an unforgivable and blasphemous act.

Iraq tried to exploit the social unrest among the Arabs of the southern oil region of Iran to wreck Khomeini's regime. There is little doubt that the Ba'athist regime supported elements within the Arab nationalist movement, as well as supplying Kurdish guerrilla units with arms, munitions and other materials.[2] Furthermore, all the right-wing organisations and groups that sought to overthrow Khomeini were welcomed and supported by the Iraqi state. For example, the ex-Shah's premier Bakhtiyar and his supporters, as well as General Oveissi and his armed gang, were given a base of operations, financial aid, and help with establishing their own radio stations.

In October 1979, following Shi'ite demonstrations in Bahrain, Kuwait and Saudi Arabia, Saddam Hussein warned, 'Iraq's capabilities can be used against any side which tries to violate the sovereignty of Kuwait or Bahrain or harm their people or land. This applies to the entire Gulf.'[3] This signalled an intensification of the propaganda war between the two regimes. Negotiations between the two sides were abandoned when Islamic Revolutionary

Guards attacked the Iraqi embassy in Tehran, the consulate at Khorramshahr, and occupied the Iraqi consulate in Kermanshah.

By December the number and severity of border clashes had escalated to such an extent that there were regular, almost daily, hostilities between Iraqi and Iranian forces. There existed, in effect, a state of undeclared war between the two countries.

During the first half of 1980 the undeclared war was intensified by both sides, with repeated air strikes, cross-border raids, artillery skirmishes, and so on. Until this time there had been two principal factors preventing outright war. Despite its propaganda about 'exporting the Islamic revolution' the Iranian regime was still consolidating its hold over Iranian society. Militarily weak after the near collapse of the armed forces, the regime was riven with factional disputes and already involved in a regional war with the Kurds that was draining its financial and military resources. It was therefore hardly in a position to declare war on Iraq and was content to continue this conflict at the level of cross-border skirmishes. This degree of military involvement was sufficient to divert public attention from internal problems, especially the conflict with the Kurds, and would give the regime enough time to consolidate its power and perhaps instigate an uprising in Iraq itself.

The Iraqi regime was militarily in a far better position, although it had to take into account the position of Syria, its implacable enemy. Until mid-1980 Iraq still hoped for, (and probably worked towards) the overthrow of Khomeini's regime by means of a coup. In June, Khomeini's forces thwarted an attempted coup by police, army and navy officers in Khuzistan, and elements of the air force based near Tehran. Iraq then realised that it must resort to other means. It was obvious that President Assad of Syria was fully diverted by internal social unrest and the Lebanon. Iraq therefore had little to worry about from that quarter. To remove the threat posed by Khomeini and to install a 'friendly' government, the Islamic republic would have to be destroyed from without.

It seems that from June 1980 onwards, Saddam Hussein began to prepare for an invasion of south-western Iran. If Saddam Hussein could destroy the Islamic republic not only would he remove the threat of Khomeini inspired Shi'ite rebellion within Iraq, but he would also establish Iraq as a regional power comparable to Iran in the Shah's heyday. On 5 August, he made his first state visit to Saudi Arabia, ostensibly to discuss the Israeli annexation of Jerusalem, but in reality to assess the attitude of the Saudi rulers towards war with Iran. The financial, political and diplomatic support of Saudi Arabia was essential. Although the Saudi rulers were extremely anxious and had great reservations, Saddam Hussein seems to have gained their support. After an agreement with North Yemen, the Gulf states and King Hussein of Jordan, Saddam Hussein received assurances that in the event of war with Iran they would assist Iraq and underwrite Iraq's risks.[4]

The invasion plan – which never envisaged the total conquest of Iran – was prepared in Baghdad with the assistance of Iran's former military and SAVAK officers and with the full agreement of Bakhtiyar and General Oveissi.[5] According to intelligence reports submitted to the Iranian authorities, the Iraqi military command intended to seize Khuzestan in less than a week and establish a 'free government' there, headed by Bakhtiyar.[6] This surprise offensive was to coincide with three other developments: a mass uprising against the Islamic regime by the Arab population of the oil region (who would theoretically join forces with the Iraqi invaders); a revolt by the supposedly disenchanted officers and men within the armed forces and the fall of Kurdistan into the hands of the Kurdish guerrillas and the establishment of a link between them and the 'free government' of Khuzestan.[7]

The calculations behind the plan seemed, on paper, to be sound. Despite the purges that had been carried out it is likely that there were elements in the armed forces who would, given the chance, rise up against the Islamic regime. The Arab nationalists had already shown their willingness to rise against Khomeini; and Kurdistan was certainly in a state of rebellion.

However, what the planners lacked was any real understanding of the Islamic revolution itself. This meant that the plan did not take into account four fundamental factors: the power of Islamic ideology which was rooted in the very fabric of Iranian society; the dedication and commitment of much of the Iranian population to the person of Khomeini; Iranian patriotism, which was very strongly felt by all sections of society, including the armed forces; and the unwillingness of the Kurdish guerrillas and the Arab population in general to join a Ba'athist-installed Bakhtiyar government, or for that matter to support Iraqi invasion, given that their compatriots – Kurds and Shi'ite Arabs – had suffered greatly under the Ba'athist regime.

On 18 September 1980 Iraq announced that it was taking control of the Shatt al-Arab estuary and abrogating the 1975 Algiers Pact. On 22 September the border conflict between Iraq and Iran turned into full-scale war. The invasion of Khuzestan had begun. Iraqi MiG fighters swept deep into Iran attacking 10 civilian and military airports (including Mehrabad, near Tehran), and bombed Iranian early-warning radar stations at night.

Iraq initially invaded five strategically important points. In the north, between Qasr-e-Shirin and Naft-e-Shah, Iraqis crossed the border in divisional strength (20,000 men), headed towards the provincial capital of Kermanshah and neutralised the airbase there. This protected the route to Baghdad and eliminated a persistent source of artillery attack. Somewhat further south, they attacked and captured the area around Mehran. Still further south they headed towards the important town of Dezful with its large airbase and all-important pumping station for the pipelines linking the southern oil fields to Tehran. Just north of the Gulf they headed for Ahwaz, the capital of Khuzestan; and finally, on the Gulf itself, they attacked the port town of Khorramshahr and the oil refinery town of Abadan.

The Iraqi air strikes on Iran's oil sources – the Abadan refineries and the oil terminal at Kharg Island – forced Iran to suspend all oil exports by 25 September. Counter-attacks on Iraq's oil refineries also forced Iraq to suspend oil exports through the Gulf (although it retained access to two pipelines to the Mediterranean).

On the ground, the Iraqis had perhaps a 2 to 1 advantage in manpower and the benefit of a well-organised supply line. However, in the first few days of the war it became clear that the Iranian air force had been seriously underestimated, and that it was capable of inflicting heavy damage on Iraqi installations.

As Iraq pushed towards its targets (the towns of Dezful, Ahwaz, Khorramshahr and Abadan) Baghdad realised that the roots of the Islamic revolution and the feelings of patriotism were deeper than it had assumed. The Iraqi military machine had certainly crossed the borderlands and captured hundreds of square miles of scrub and desert with ease, but the main centres in the war zone, where the people of the towns had joined forces with the Islamic Revolutionary Guards and the army, were fiercely and courageously

USSR
Caspian Sea
USSR
TURKEY
AFGHANISTAN
Tehran
Qasr-e-Shirin
Kermanshah
Naft-e-Shah
Mehran
Dezful
Baghdad
IRAN
IRAQ
Ahwaz
Khorramshahr
Abadan
Kharg Island
PAKISTAN
K.
Persian Gulf
B.
Q.
SAUDI ARABIA
UAE
OMAN

resisting the invaders. Even the supposedly shattered Iranian air force had consistently out-performed and out-manoeuvred its opposite number.

By 30 September 1980 the rapid Iraqi advance across the Khuzestan plain had been brought to a halt and the Iraqi war timetable badly disrupted. In early October, Iraq had to withdraw at least 20,000 troops from their camps in northern (Iraqi) Kurdistan and move them to the south.[8]

The battle for Khorramshahr and Abadan

By mid-October the Iraqis had only reached the outskirts of Khuzestan's principal towns. The fall of Khorramshahr was essential, since beyond Khorramshahr lay three possible prizes: the refinery town of Abadan, vital to the full control of the Shatt al-Arab waterways; Ahwaz, the capital of the oil region; and a possible corridor connecting Iraq's northern forces with its southern divisions. After days of artillery bombardment, which had turned Khorramshahr into a scrapyard, a ragged Iranian force of civilian volunteers, Islamic Revolutionary Guards and regular soldiers, doggedly stood its ground.

By this time the towns of Khorramshahr and Abadan were virtually cut off from the rest of the country. The end of October saw Khorramshahr's last hours of siege. As the Iraqi forces moved in from the suburbs towards the centre, the defenders sent out desperate appeals for military assistance, water, food, ammunition and weapons. Unable to come to their aid, the clerical authorities urged the defenders 'to go out and drink "the nectar of martyrs" with a clear conscience'.[9]

The fall of Khorramshahr, however, came too late for the Iraqis to achieve their objectives of capturing Abadan and Ahwaz to establish a link between their southern and northern forces. By mid-November, although they had besieged the towns of Abadan and Ahwaz, the Iraqi military machine was forced into a slow-moving war of attrition. Their military strategy of mobile warfare had to be changed to that of siege warfare.

If the battle of Khorramshahr forced a change in the Iraqi strategy, the long siege of Abadan (from October 1980 to September 1981) eventually transformed the outlook of the war itself. In Abadan the inhabitants, under a constant barrage of Iraqi artillery from almost all sides, fought off all attempts to break their defensive position. As oil and dock installations burned and shanty towns and streets were bombed to the ground, young and old feverishly dug trenches and built barricades. For the most part the defenders of Abadan were aged between 16 and 20, but reports also mention boys of 13 and 14 fighting beside their fathers.[10]

The war moved into a second phase. The defence of Abadan provided the Iranian forces with much-needed time to regroup, and to move tanks and artillery to block the likely routes of any future Iraqi advance. A stalemate resulted. From then on, until the unsuccessful Iranian offensive at Susangerd (south of Dezful) in February 1981, there was hardly any movement in the war. This was a period of murderous artillery battles, barrages of surface-to-surface missiles, and trench warfare. It had become a classic war of attrition, devastating the towns of Ahwaz, Dezful and Abadan, where almost the only people left were armed young men. Once the Iraqis had failed to achieve their original military objectives they seem to have put their effort into terrorising the fleeing population. While the West was preoccupied with its future oil supplies, war was wreaking havoc in the towns and villages of this oil-rich region.

The Iranian offensive: a turning point

At the end of September 1981 the Iranian forces launched a successful counter-attack to break the siege of Abadan. It took some 12 hours of fierce combat to push the Iraqi forces to the western side of the Karun River. This success did little to alter the military stalemate, as the Iranians failed to take advantage of the Iraqi retreat to recapture Khorramshahr. For this they apparently needed more time to prepare. In the meantime, they concentrated on the small town of Bostan, 10 miles from Iraq's border in the centre of the war front.

The recapture of Bostan boosted the morale of the Iranians who took about 2,000 prisoners and captured scores of tanks and armoured vehicles. The Bostan operation, code-named *Fathelfotuh* ('victory of victories') was carried out by combined forces of the regular army and Islamic Revolutionary Guards. Their way through the minefields was cleared by raw teenage recruits who volunteered as human minesweepers in the name of Islam.

However, the Iranian forces failed, due to a heavy counter-attack by the Iraqis, to reach the border which would have split the Iraqi forces in two.

The capture of Bostan was the start of a radical change in the outlook of the war. An Iranian offensive, code-named *Fatholmobin* ('blessed victory'), was launched the day after the Iranian New Year, on 22 March 1982. This finally broke the stalemate and the war entered its third phase. The immediate aim of the Iranian offensive was to free the territory around Dezful and Shush. In a week of heavy fighting the Iranian forces defeated the Iraqi Fourth Army. A human wave of volunteers (recruited to the war by the *Basij* (Mobilisation) Organisation) provided the main thrust of the offensive, with the teenage volunteers repeatedly throwing themselves at the Iraqi lines, and regular soldiers and Islamic Revolutionary Guards moving in behind them.

The Iraqi Fourth Army suffered heavily, with at least 5,000 dead or wounded and 15,000 taken prisoner. The Iranians also paid a heavy price for this victory – over 7,000 dead, most of them teenage volunteers. Yet there was no shortage of others to take their place. As one commentator put it, 'This readiness to die so baffled some Iraqis that they attributed it to drugs administered by the Mullahs.'[11]

A large number of the *Basij* volunteers died for their belief in Islam and their dedication to Khomeini. But not all the teenage fighters[12] were so dedicated to the cause of Islam. Many were drafted into the war and fought simply to survive with no ideals of martyrdom. As a 16-year-old Iranian prisoner of war told a Western reporter, 'I was a student in school in Tehran and they [the clergy-controlled *Basij* Organisation] forced me to come to fight. I was captured today. It was my first fight.'[13]

The March offensive forced the Iraqis to change their war policy. On 11 April 1982, Saddam declared that the main aim of the war was to prevent an Iranian invasion of Iraqi territory. An Islamic 'peace mission' repeatedly failed in its attempts to bring the two sides to the negotiating table. The Tehran authorities, under orders from Khomeini, refused to meet the Iraqis until the latter accepted certain conditions: the complete withdrawal of all Iraqi troops; war reparations (sometimes put as high as $150bn); the setting up of an international tribunal to 'investigate and punish the aggressor'; the admission of war guilt by Iraq; and the repatriation of 100,000 Iraqi Shi'ites then in Iran. These conditions were so humiliating that their acceptance would be political suicide for Saddam Hussein and his regime.

Three major campaigns by Iran in the second half of 1982 pushed the Iraqi forces out of Khorramshahr and the Iranian territory occupied since September 1980, except for five pockets in the border area – about 130 square miles – around the oil fields of Naft-e-Shahr and Shalamcheh near Khorramshahr. The offensives began in early summer with an operation code-named *Ramadan* which, after the recapture of Khorramshahr, placed a huge Iranian force of infantry and tanks on the border with Iraq. This threatened the narrow waist of southern Iraq and aimed to isolate Iraq's second city of Basra. For the first time in this war Iranian forces were fighting beyond their own borders. The Iraqi regime announced in June 1982 that it was withdrawing from Iranian territory, except for the five pockets on the border which it claimed should have been returned to it under the 1975 Algiers Treaty. Iran seemed unconcerned about these disputed areas and launched no major offensive to retake them. Indeed, their continued occupation provided a convenient pretext for attacking the Iraqis over the border.

In October 1982 operation *Muharram* was launched, ostensibly to recapture these pockets of territory, but in reality, to enter Iraq. On 7 November the Iranian forces penetrated some four to seven miles into the Iraqi border area of Misan, but then the attack became bogged down.

In all these operations the Iranians relied heavily on their tactic of mass suicide. Wave after wave of young volunteer martyrs were mown down by Iraqi troops, their corpses littering the battlefields; 'some no older than 13 bore the brunt of the early fighting, throwing themselves upon Iraqi guns and opening the way for the regular soldiers'.[14] By October 1982, between 70,000 and 100,000 Iranians and at least 30,000 Iraqis had been killed in the war.[15] There are more than 45,000 Iraqi prisoners of war in the hands of the Islamic regime and some 5,000 Iranians held by Iraq.[16]

The impact of the war on Iran

The human misery caused by the war has been immense, especially in Iran where the war has created at least 2 million refugees.[17]

According to the Iranian Interior Ministry, there are 20 tent cities to accommodate refugees, but most have moved to the main inner-urban centres. It is estimated that only 30 per cent of refugees live in the tent cities.[18] The problem of coping with the refugees is immense in itself, and has aggravated the already severe social and economic crisis in Iran. The migration to the cities has resulted in shortages of food and other necessities, as well as widespread homelessness in the urban centres.

The reconstruction of the devastated south-western region will take years to accomplish and consume billions of dollars of state investment. The war itself is costing the Islamic republic more than $500 million a month.[19] This immense financial burden has deepened the economic crisis and reduced state investment drastically.

Although the impact of the war on the economy, coupled with the social problem of war refugees, has created intolerable living conditions for the working population, so far the regime has been able to sustain its political and ideological hegemony. In fact, rather than weaken the Islamic regime the war allowed it to strengthen its hold over Iranian society. Initially at least, the regime benefited from a surge of patriotism and was able to mobilise the bulk of the population in support of its struggle against an alleged US–Israeli conspiracy to smash the Islamic revolution. Even among the national and ethnic minorities, including the Arabs of the oil region, patriotism and unity against the invader were dominant. Thousands of people volunteered to fight, including members of some left-wing organisations such as the Fedayeen guerrillas, who fought side-by-side with their future executioners, the Islamic Revolutionary Guards.

The war was used not only to divert attention from internal economic, social and political problems, but also to accelerate the consolidation of clerical power, while providing the regime with the opportunity of pursuing its aim of the 'export of the Islamic revolution'.

Thanks largely to Iraqi invasion, the regime's apparatus of repression had been greatly strengthened. Organisations such as the Islamic Revolutionary Guards, the *Basij*, and the security and intelligence agencies have rapidly matured and become efficient instruments of power.

The militant clergy used the war to give prominence to irregular forces, especially the Islamic Revolutionary Guards. This was particularly important during the period before the ousting of Bani-Sadr. While he attempted to promote the cause of the armed forces, the militant clergy was building the Islamic Revolutionary Guards, entrusting to them the defence of the besieged cities and villages and reducing the role of the regular army. The whole conduct of the war was at that time influenced by the internal power struggle in the Islamic regime, and the military failures of 1980 and 1981 were used against Bani-Sadr by the Islamic Republican Party.

The Islamic Revolutionary Guards, or *Pasdaran*, numbered about 30,000 before the war. They soon intensified their recruiting drive in the cities and villages, training and arming devout Moslems. They established their own general staff, separate from the Iranian armed forces, to co-ordinate and organise their military operations, and purchased their own arms, sometimes directly from Libya and Syria. They founded their own intelligence service and public relations offices and produced regular publications to propagate their political platform. The war gave them invaluable military experience.

By 1981, the *Pasdaran* organisation had grown to become a fully established paramilitary force of some 200,000 trained commandos with perhaps as many as a million more undergoing training.[20] The mosque also mobilised for the war through the *Basij* organisation, which recruited the many teenagers who were to die at the head of Iranian offensives. The *Basij* was also involved in organising civil defence teams and planned to set up 46 summer camps for political, ideological and military training for this purpose.[21]

With the ousting of Bani-Sadr and the defeat of the liberals, the clergy extended its control over the regular armed forces. The intention of the militant clergy had always been to Islamicise the military machine left by the Shah. The *Pasdaran* paramilitary force was never intended to replace the regular forces. The military purges of 1979 and 1980[22] were not intended to dissolve the army but to mould it into an Islamic framework and to prevent it ever again becoming a politically dominant force.

There is little doubt that the army has become a highly efficient fighting force, loyal to its masters in Tehran, and particularly to Khomeini. The war, which necessitated a high level of co-ordination between the paramilitary, *Basij* and regular armed forces, has provided the Islamic regime with a powerful and experienced military machine. Once the war has ended, the army's future deployment will probably be limited to dealing with large-scale rebellions, such as in Kurdistan, and the defence of the realm, rather than internal suppression. The army could, however, play a decisive role in a future internal power struggle between different Islamic tendencies.

The Islamic Revolutionary Guards (*Pasdaran*) have also undoubtedly benefited from the experience of war. Their future role will not only be to supplement the functions of the regular forces, but also, and this is their fundamental role, to combat internal subversion. The *Pasdaran* will continue to be agents of repression. They have already planned to set up a training academy offering a three-year course in ideological, political and military matters.[23] The creation of a Revolutionary Guards Ministry has completed the institutionalisation of this force. Its existence complicates any future plans for a coup by the regular armed forces because the Islamic Revolutionary Guards control the streets and could turn any coup attempt into a civil war.

Although the regime has used the war to accelerate the institutionalisation of clerical power by channelling Islamic fervour and Iranian patriotism towards its own ends, there are signs that attitudes are changing. The regime has been faced, at least since it has no longer been fighting for Iranian territory, with difficulties in recruiting to the armed forces, especially in the central and northern provinces, and more particularly in the urban areas. An indication of the regime's concern about draft-dodging is a proposal for 70 amendments to the Conscription Act. Anyone eligible for military service[24] would have to obtain exemption before being allowed to obtain a loan, stand for election, receive a school diploma, register a business or property, work in a government department, or even take a driving test. Draft-dodgers would be denied access to such activities for 10 years. What is more, they would be refused all public utilities – water, electricity, gas or telephone services.[25]

Although signs of dissatisfaction with the regime exist, and give the opposition cause for optimism, they are far from sufficient to unseat the clergy. The road towards that goal is undoubtedly arduous, painful and bloody.

Regional implications of the war

Despite repeated rejections of the peace mission's proposals, there are those within the Islamic hierarchy who would prefer a swift end to the war with Iraq. Khomeini, however, is still demanding the overthrow of the Ba'athist regime. In February 1983 another offensive by Iranian forces was launched. Even if this were able to capture Baghdad and bring down the Ba'athist regime, which is unlikely, such a move would have far-reaching regional and international ramifications.

Iraq invaded Iran only after it had obtained solid Arab backing. A mutual defence agreement was signed in June 1980 by Iraq and Jordan. The Gulf states also supported Iraq politically and financially, as well as providing military aid and sanctuary for Iraqi forces. There have been reports that Sudan has offered to send troops to aid Iraq and that during autumn 1982 Iraq received at least 45 Egyptian pilots.[26] A full-scale invasion of Iraq would, therefore, intensify the Gulf war rather than end it, and would probably transform the pact between the Gulf states and Iraq into a new military alliance.

According to US sources, military aid has been flowing to Iran from Soviet client states or allies such as North Korea, Vietnam, Libya and Syria.[27] However, much of Iran's weaponry is purchased on the international arms market, largely from Western Europe.[28] The unofficial arms trade between Israel and Iran has been going on for some time, in fact, since the Carter administration.[29] Israel's willingness to sell arms to the Khomeini regime was not principally due to commercial considerations; it was a political decision. As far as Israel was concerned, the worst outcome of the war would have been a clear-cut Iraqi victory, enhancing Saddam's aspirations as a hard-line leader of the Arabs.

Whatever the final outcome of the war, it has altered the balance of power in the Gulf. If Iran can maintain its present position it can force a humiliating settlement on Iraq. Iraq's bid to become the gendarme of the Gulf has failed, and its position within the Arab world has been downgraded. Its war machine is exhausted and successive defeats have demoralised its military and political establishments. This may lead to internal Shi'ite upheavals and, perhaps, renewed rebellion in (Iraqi) Kurdistan. As the Kurds in Iran are still struggling against Khomeini, this would, for the first time in Kurdish history, give a united Kurdistan a chance to achieve nationhood. Such a move would create further conflicts in the region: for example, in Turkey, which holds a part of Kurdish territory.

The conflict between Iran and Iraq is more than a 'local war'. It is waged in a region which is highly volatile, and riven with divisions. It is a region of vital economic and strategic importance to the major world powers who are already indirectly involved. Their direct involvement is unlikely at the moment but any assessment of the future of the Middle East, particularly the Gulf area, must take into account the impact of the Iraq–Iran war.

Conclusion

The dominant role of Islam in the Iranian revolution of 1979 was neither accidental nor superficial. The Islamic revolution resulted from the specific social, economic and political conditions of Iranian society. Although the reforms and economic development pushed through under the Shah seemed to have lessened the influence of Islam over the mass of the population, in reality the opposite was true. The reforms had created the very conditions that provided Islam with its strong social base.

The Shah's reforms and moves towards capitalist development disrupted the traditional class structure, producing social classes in a state of transition. By breaking up the old rural social order these reforms freed huge numbers of people from traditional economic and community ties who could not possibly be absorbed by Iranian industry at its existing stage of development. With their class status as yet undetermined, their social consciousness belonged to a past mode of life while their objective conditions marked their future as a proletarian mass. It was the urban poor, the new recruits to the working class, that fought and built the Islamic revolution and that continues to keep Khomeini in power.

The majority of the urban petty bourgeoisie was also in a transitional state. Despite state intervention which encroached upon the traditional activities of this class, it has managed to preserve its traditional domain, the bazaar.

The working class was a class in the process of making itself. It was not sufficiently organised to recognise or assert its own independent class power. It was certainly a class 'in itself' but had yet to become a class 'for itself'.

None of the mass classes – the urban petty bourgeoisie, the working class and the urban poor – saw their own power as the means of achieving their aims. Each felt themselves to be so weak that they relied on 'patronage from above' to fulfil their interests.

After 25 years of repressive dictatorship, a political vacuum existed so it was not surprising that the mosque and the clergy were able to take on this role. Islamic ideology became a substitute for the lost communality of the oppressed masses. In the mosque, with its nationwide organisational network, the masses sought the power that would liberate them from the Shah's dictatorship, not recognising that this power was their own.

Khomeini's personal role in this should not be underestimated. It was in him that diverse social groups and classes saw their long-awaited saviour. While social and political conditions generated the circumstances that would allow a patriarchal figure immense influence, it was Khomeini's political astuteness that enabled him to present himself as the only alternative to the Shah. In a society riddled with corrupt, inconsistent and weak politicians, Khomeini presented himself as incorruptible, uncompromising and sincere. To the militant clergy and the oppressed masses he came to represent the personification of divine authority, shepherding the masses towards freedom, and unity with God.

Khomeini and the militant clergy led the revolution, with the mosque and the bazaar providing organisational and financial support. Although the intelligentsia sparked off the revolution and guerrilla fighters struck the final blows, the revolution never really belonged to them; they neither organised nor led it, but followed Khomeini and the militant clergy from the start of the revolution to its end – the triumph of reaction.

The urban poor provided the infantry and the cannon-fodder of the Islamic revolution; the working class was its battering ram. The working class, despite its crucial role, entered the scene of revolution not as an independent force but subserviently, unconscious of its historic responsibility and potential. The working class can only teach itself the art of revolution through its own struggle, and, in Iran, those struggles were both recent and limited, localised and fragmented.

The Islamic revolution was a political rather than a social revolution, led and finally won by a reactionary social layer, the clergy. The revolutionary upheavals of 1977–79 contained within them the forces of reaction, in spite of the genuine anti-imperialist and democratic aspirations of the masses. To the extent that the Islamic movement was forced by political conditions to stress its character as a movement of the oppressed, it was anti-authoritarian and revolutionary. However, to the extent that it consistently asserted its fundamental objective to be the creation of an Islamic order, it was authoritarian and reactionary. These two contradictory aspects were both represented in the Islamic movement during the events of 1977–79.

Khomeini did not betray the revolution, for the revolution was his and the clergy's; he betrayed the aspirations of the masses who followed him. Khomeini's seizure of power was no counter-revolution, but the consolidation of victorious Islamic reaction. In terms of social and economic development, the Islamic regime is undoubtedly retrogressive. Its fundamental aim is to establish the supremacy of Islam which is not just a religion but an inherently anti-democratic political system. The struggle against Khomeini's regime, the struggle for democracy, is inseparable from the struggle against Islam as a political, social, legal and ideological system.

Notes and references

1. Foreign domination

1. See C. Issawi (ed.), *The Economic History of Iran 1800–1914*, University of Chicago 1971, p. 335.
2. On the Reuter Concession see F. Kazemzadeh, *Russia and Britain in Persia, 1864–1914, A Study in Imperialism*, Yale University Press 1968, pp. 103*ff*; also L. E. Frechtling, 'The Reuter Concession in Persia', *The Asiatic Review*, vol. 34 no. 119, July 1938, pp. 518–33.
3. See N. R. Keddie, *Religion and Rebellion in Iran: The Tobacco Protest of 1891–1892*, London: Frank Cass 1966, and A. K. S. Lambton, 'The tobacco regie: prelude to revolution', I and II, *Studia Islamica*, vol. 22, 1969, pp. 70–90, 119–157.
4. L. P. Elwell-Sutton, *Persian Oil: A Study in Power Politics*, London: Lawrence & Wishart 1955, p. 84; W. H. Bartsch gives a figure of £120 million, see 'The impact of the oil industry on the economy of Iran', in R. F. Mikesell, *Foreign Investment in the Petroleum and Mineral Industries*, Baltimore: Johns Hopkins Press 1971, p. 246.
5. Elwell-Sutton, *op. cit.* pp. 99–101.
6. *ibid.* pp. 96–97.
7. *ibid.* p. 88.
8. *ibid.* pp. 88–89.
9. See G. Lenczowski, *Oil and State in the Middle East*, Cornell University Press 1960, p. 262.

2. Economic development

1. See N. S. Fatemi, *Diplomatic History of Persia 1917–1923: Anglo-Russian Power Politics in Iran*, New York: Russel F. Moore 1952, p. 11; also J. M. Balfour, *Recent Happenings in Persia*, Edinburgh: Blackwood & Sons 1922, pp. 123–25.
2. See H. W. V. Temperley, *A History of the Peace Conference of Paris*, VI, London: Hodder & Stoughton 1920–24, p. 210.

3. See H. Katouzian, *The Political Economy of Modern Iran 1926–1979*, London: Macmillan 1981, p. 75.
4. Between 1932 and 1938 all eight sugar refineries established were state-owned; J. Bharier, *Economic Development in Iran 1900–1970*, Oxford University Press 1971, p. 176.
5. *ibid.* pp. 176, 178.
6. *ibid.* p. 172.
7. See L. P. Elwell-Sutton, *Modern Iran*, London: George Routledge & Sons 1941, p. 112.
8. On state control of foreign trade see S. Simmonds, *Economic Conditions in Iran (Persia)*, London: Department of Overseas Trade 1935, p. 15.
9. See Bharier, *op. cit.* p. 86.
10. See H. Motamen, 'Development planning in Iran', *Middle East Economic Papers*, 1956, pp. 103–4; a planning board was set up in fact, in April 1946, *ibid.* p. 98.
11. Bharier, *op. cit.* p. 90.
12. L. P. Elwell-Sutton, *Persian Oil: A Study in Power Politics*, London: Lawrence & Wishart 1955, p. 185.
13. J. Stork, 'Middle East oil and the energy crisis', *Monthly Review Press*, New York and London: 1975, p. 53.
14. A. Sampson, *The Seven Sisters*, London: Coronet Books 1977, pp. 135–36.
15. There was a secret agreement on the purchase of oil and restriction of its production to avoid a glut, see *ibid.* pp. 145–46.
16. See F. Halliday, *Iran: Dictatorship and Development*, Harmondsworth: Penguin Books 1979; the rates of duty levied on imports were in some cases as high as 200–300 per cent, and the average was about 80 per cent, *ibid.* p. 150; in the automobile industry it had reached 500 per cent.
17. *ibid.* p. 153.
18. See Kayhan Research Associates, *A Guide to Iran's 5th Plan 1973–1978*, Tehran: no date, p. 19.
19. H. Askari and S. Majin, 'Recent economic growth in Iran', *Middle Eastern Studies*, (Special Issue), vol. 12 no. 3, October 1976, p. 107.
20. C. Issawi, 'Growth and structural change in the Middle East', *The Middle East Journal*, vol. 25 no. 3, 1971, p. 318.
21. W. H. Bartsch, 'The industrial labor force of Iran: problems of recruitment, training and productivity', *The Middle East Journal*, vol. 25 no. 1, 1971, pp. 15–16.
22. Halliday, *op. cit.* p. 182.

23. J. Amouzegar and A. Fekrat, *Iran: Economic Development under Dualistic Conditions*, University of Chicago Press 1971, pp. 36–38.

24. R. Graham, *Iran: The Illusion of Power*, London: Croom Helm 1979, p. 38.

25. On the importance of oil revenue in allowing such immunity see H. Mahdavy, 'The patterns and problems of economic development in rentier states: the case of Iran', in M. A. Cook (ed.), *Studies in Economic History of the Middle East*, Oxford University Press 1970, pp. 428–67.

26. Bartsch, *op. cit.* p. 248.

27. See 'Echo of Iran', *Iran Almanac 1975*, Tehran: 1975, p. 265.

28. There were some purchases of arms from the USSR also from 1966. These were mainly of 'non-sensitive' military hardware, primarily automotive equipment such as trucks; see J. C. Hurewitz, *Middle East Politics: The Military Dimension*, London: Pall Mall Press 1969, p. 293.

29. Halliday, *op. cit.* p. 94.

30. See Stockholm International Peace Research Institute (SIPRI), *Yearbook 1978 World Armaments and Disarmament*, London: Taylor & Francis 1978, Table 8.1, p. 226.

31. *ibid.* p. 231.

32. See *ibid.* p. 217.

33. See 'Behrang', *Iran: Le Maillon Faible*, Paris: Maspero 1979, p. 85; also Halliday, *op. cit.* p. 95.

34. *Newsweek*, 14 October 1974.

35. See A. Sampson, *The Arms Bazaar*, London: Hodder & Stoughton 1977, Chapter 14, pp. 241–59; also B. Rubin, *Paved with Good Intentions: The American Experience and Iran*, Harmondsworth: Penguin Books 1981, p. 172.

36. R. K. Ramazani, *The United States and Iran: The Pattern of Influence*, New York: Praeger 1982, p. 47.

37. Rubin, *op. cit.* p. 156.

38. See the translation of Abdullaev, in C. Issawi, *The Economic History of Iran 1800–1914*, University of Chicago 1971, p. 51.

39. Bharier, *op. cit.* p. 34; Katouzian, *op. cit.* p. 259, states that it was 49 per cent for 1967–68.

40. K. McLachlan, 'Postscript', in C. Salmanzadeh, *Agricultural Change and Rural Society in Southern Iran*, Cambridge: Menas Press 1980, p. 267.

41. Bharier, *op. cit.* p. 35; Bartsch, *op. cit.* p. 17, gives the number of industrial workers as 214,307 in 1966–67.

42. Halliday, *op. cit.* p. 173.

43. 'Behrang', *op. cit.* p. 184.
44. See S. H. Schurr and P. T. Homan, *Middle Eastern Oil and the Western World, Prospects and Problems*, New York: American Elsevier 1971, p. 104.

3. Class struggle, rebellion and the clergy

1. A. K. S. Lambton, 'Secret societies and the Persian revolution of 1905–6', *St Antony's Papers*, no. 4, 1958, p. 55; see also her 'Persian political societies 1906–11', *St Antony's Papers*, no. 16, 1963, pp. 41–89.
2. On the Constitutional Revolution see E. G. Browne, *The Persian Revolution of 1905–1909*, Cambridge University Press 1910.
3. See S. Zabih, *The Communist Movement in Iran*, University of California Press 1966, pp. 13–45; also E. Abrahamian, *Iran Between Two Revolutions*, Princeton University Press 1982, p. 111.
4. See Zabih, *op. cit.*; also *Historical Documents from the Workers', Social Democratic, and Communist Movements in Iran*, Florence: Mazdak 1972, especially III, pp. 36–44. On the Gilan republic see also Fred Halliday, 'Revolution in Iran: was it possible in 1921?' *Khamsin*, no. 7, 1980, pp. 53–64.
5. See Halliday, *op. cit.* p.56.
6. See *ibid.* p. 56.
7. J. M. Upton, *The History of Modern Iran: An Interpretation*. Harvard University Press 1970, pp. 44–45; see also A. Banani, *The Modernisation of Iran 1921–1941*, Stanford University Press 1969, pp. 40–43.
8. There is no doubt that the 1921 coup was brought about with the aid and full support of the British. H. Arfa in his *Under Five Shahs*, London: John Murray 1964, mentions that after Reza Khan's initial dismissal by Colonel Staroselsky, he 'became friendly with General Dickson' who was in command of the East Persia Cordon (p. 91). Keddie states that the coup was brought about 'with British help' but was not 'ultimately British controlled', N. R. Keddie, 'The Iranian power structure and social change 1800–1969: an overview', *International Journal of Middle East Studies*, vol. 2 no. 1, January 1971, p. 10.
9. See Azar Tabari, 'Role of the Shi'i clergy in modern Iranian politics', *Kamsin*, no. 9, 1981, pp. 50–76.
10. See L. P. Elwell-Sutton, 'Political parties in Iran 1941–1948', *The Middle East Journal*, vol. 3 no. 1, 1949, pp. 45–61.
11. See E. Abrahamian, 'Communism and communalism in Iran: the

Tudah and the Firqah-i Dimukrat', *International Journal of Middle East Studies*, vol. 1 no. 4, October 1970, pp. 291–316.
12. For details of the Kurdish republic see W. Eagleton jnr, *The Kurdish Republic of 1946*, Middle Eastern Monographs: 5, Oxford University Press 1963; see also H. Arfa, *The Kurds: An Historical and Political Study*, Oxford University Press 1966; and A. R. Ghassemlou, 'Iranian Kurdistan', a pamphlet, no date.
13. See E. Abrahamian, 'The crowd in Iranian politics 1905–1953', *Past and Present*, no. 41, December 1968, pp. 189–190.
14. See F. Halliday, 'Iran: trade unions and the working class opposition', *Middle East Research and Information Project Reports*, no. 71, October 1978, p. 10.
15. For the Mossadeq period, see B. Nirumand, 'Iran; the new imperialism in action', *Monthly Review Press*, New York: 1969; also S. Zabih, *The Mossadegh Era: Roots of the Iranian Revolution*, Chicago: Lake View Press 1982.

4. The consolidation of dictatorship

1. The pro-Mossadeq officers were informed about Nasiri's move by the Tudeh Party's secret military network.
2. On CIA activity see A. Tully, *CIA: The Inside Story*, New York: Simon & Schuster 1962; also K. Roosevelt, *Countercoup: The Struggle for the Control of Iran*, New York: McGraw-Hill 1979, and his article, 'How the CIA brought the Shah to power', *Washington Post*, 6 May 1979. See also F. J. Cook, 'The CIA', *The Nation*, vol. 192, 1961, p. 529.
3. On the Tudeh Party see E. Abrahamian's excellent study in his *Iran: Between Two Revolutions*, Princeton University Press 1982, Chapter 6, 7 and 8, pp. 281–415.
4. The CIA agent Kermit Roosevelt (head of operations in Iran at the time of the coup) mentions that 'certain Israeli friends discreetly joined the CIA in helping to organise and give guidance to a new Iranian Security Service', see Roosevelt, *op. cit.* p. 9.
5. It must be noted that the structure of international capitalism, with the growth of great concentrations of capital in the hands of Western industrial powers, made the tasks of Mossadeq's government contradictory; the accumulation of capital, national independence and the socialisation of labour were mutually inconsistent. Mossadeq failed to resolve this contradiction. The Pahlavi dictatorship aimed to do so by means of reforms (through

distribution of the oil revenue) and entrance into the world market. The creation of a 'social base' is the resolution of the above contradiction. The reforms that the dictatorship aimed to carry out were, in fact, not exclusive to Iran. During the Kennedy administration the US had embarked on a general policy of reforms and industrialisation for third world countries under its influence. For an understanding of the contradictions of Mossadeq's period see Razi, 'Concerning revolutionary programme and manner', *Kavosh*, 1st year no. 2, pp. 4–6.

6. See F. Halliday, *Iran: Dictatorship and Development*, Harmondsworth: Penguin 1979, p. 111; for a detailed study of the land reform in Iran (in its early stages) see A. K. S. Lambton, *The Persian Land Reform 1962–66*, Oxford: Clarendon Press 1969.

7. See E. Hooglund, 'Iran's agricultural inheritance', *Middle East Research and Information Project Reports*, September 1981, p. 16.

8. Iranian agriculture was always dominated by the village community system and not a peasantry system of smallholders.

9. P. Ghorayshi, 'Capitalism in rural Iran', *Middle East Research and Information Project Reports*, no. 98, July–August 1981, p. 29.

10. See M. Dobb, 'From feudalism to capitalism', in R. Hilton, *The Transition from Feudalism to Capitalism*, London: NLB 1976, p. 165. The Iranian state's general agrarian policy, especially its irrigation policy, favouring 'the needs of the large-scale units', as Ghorayshi, *op. cit.* p. 29 mentions, and virtually ignoring 'the desperate need of the smaller ones', clearly demonstrates the real intentions of a ruthless capitalist state in the promotion and expansion of capitalism by promoting the conditions for the eventual uprooting of the smallholders and the transformation of these into (potential) wage-labourers.

11. See K. McLachlan, 'Postscript', in C. Salmanzadeh, *Agricultural Change and Rural Society in Southern Iran*, Cambridge: Menas Press 1980, p. 267.

12. This is precisely why US advisers – especially during the Kennedy administration – not only encouraged the implementation of land reform in Iran, but helped supervise it.

13. N. R. Keddie, *Roots of Revolution*, Yale University Press 1981, p. 156.

14. In March 1963, the Iranian Foreign Ministry advised the USA that diplomatic privileges were approved for senior US military advisers. On 13 October 1964, the Shah's parliament approved the extension of diplomatic privileges to US military personnel thus exempting them from criminal and civil jurisdiction. For details see R. Pfau,

'The legal status of American forces in Iran', *The Middle East Journal*, vol. 28 no. 2, 1974, pp. 141–53.
15. See E. Abrahamian, *Iran Between Two Revolutions*, Princeton University Press 1982, p. 426.
16. See B. Rubin, *Paved With Good Intentions: The American Experience and Iran*, Harmondsworth: Penguin Books 1981, p. 109.
17. See for example, Resurgence Party's Handbook, *The Philosophy of Iran's Revolution*, Tehran: 1976.
18. M. M. J. Fischer, *Iran: From Religious Dispute to Revolution*, Harvard University Press 1980, p. 125.

5. The social forces of opposition

1. R. Graham, *Iran: The Illusion of Power*, London: Croom Helm 1979, p. 224.
2. *ibid.* p. 224.
3. See Bank Markazi (Central Bank), *Annual Report*, Tehran: 1974–75, p. 74.
4. See E. Abrahamian, 'Iran: the political challenge', *MERIP Reports*, no. 69, July–August 1978, p. 4.
5. See M. Field (ed.), 'Middle East Annual Report', *The Economist*, 1977, pp. 150–58; see also H. Katouzian, *The Political Economy of Modern Iran 1926–1979*, London: Macmillan 1981, p. 334, where it is mentioned that the middle classes 'had to pay 50 per cent of their salaries for the rental of a five-room apartment'.
6. N. R. Keddie, 'The Iranian village before and after land reform', *Journal of Contemporary History*, 3 July 1968, p. 86; see also F. Khamsi, 'Land Reform in Iran', *Monthly Review*, 21 June 1969, p. 28.
7. M. A. Katouzian, 'Oil versus agriculture: a case of dual resource depletion in Iran', *Journal of Peasant Studies*, 5 August 1978, p. 361.
8. For example, the ratio of urban to rural income per head was estimated in 1959 as 4.6 to 1, which had increased by 1969 to 4.7 to 1, see F. Kazemi, *Poverty and Revolution in Iran*, New York University Press 1980, p. 42. The daily wage in 1972 of a male agricultural worker was $1.40 and of a female worker 75 cents. This was several times lower than the wage of an unskilled contruction worker in the cities in the same period, see Kazemi, *ibid.* p. 42.
9. *ibid.* p. 43.
10. *ibid.* p. 55.
11. *ibid.* p. 50.
12. *ibid.* p. 50.

13. *ibid.* p. 51.
14. H. Katouzian, *op. cit.* p. 335.
15. See *ibid.* note 3, p. 352.
16. *ibid.* p. 336.
17. See Kazemi, *op. cit.* p. 108.
18. F. Halliday, 'Iran: economic contradictions', *Middle East Research and Information Project Reports*, no. 69, July–August 1978, p. 11.
19. F. Halliday, 'Iran: trade unions and the working class opposition', *Middle East Research and Information Project Reports*, no. 71, October 1978, p. 12. For the attitude of the business community see the *Tehran Economist*, 22 May 1976, pp. 4–5
20. See 'Behrang', *Iran: Le maillon faible*, Paris: Maspero 1979, p. 264.
21. Halliday, *op. cit.* p. 12.
22. 'Survey of Iran', *Financial Times*, 25 July 1977.
23. See Halliday, *op. cit.* p. 12.
24. See T. Jalil, *Workers of Iran: Repression and the Fight for Democratic Trade Unions*, Campaign for the Restoration of Trade Union Rights in Iran, London: July 1976, p. 56.
25. See 'Behrang', *op. cit.* p. 280.
26. For more details see the table of strikes in *ibid.* pp. 270–94.
27. See Halliday, *op. cit.* p. 12.

6. From protest to revolution

1. According to Ramazani, 'An intelligence report during the Republican administration [Nixon's], made only weeks before the change of administration, asserted that Iran was likely to remain stable under the Shah over the next several years . . . that the chances were good that Iran would have relatively little trouble until at least the mid-1980s'. R. K. Ramazani, *The United States and Iran*, New York: Praeger 1982, p. 126.
2. See Amnesty International, *Report 1974–75*, London: 1975; and P. Jacobson, 'Torture in Iran', *Sunday Times*, 19 January 1975.
3. See International Commission of Jurists, 'Human rights and the legal system in Iran', Geneva: 1976, pp. 1–72.
4. In August 1977, a US intelligence report stated that the Shah 'will be an active participant in Iranian life well into the 1980s'; and as Ramazani has shown even 'eight months after the start of the disturbances, a better known intelligence study asserted in its preface that Iran "is not a revolutionary situation"' ', Subcommittee on Evaluation, Permanent Select Committee on Intelligence, US Congress, Staff Report, see Ramazani, *op. cit.* pp. 126–27.

5. E. Abrahamian, *Iran Between Two Revolutions*, Princeton University Press 1982, p. 500.
6. See M. R. Pahlavi, *Answer to History*, New York: Stein & Day 1980, p. 150.
7. B. Rubin, *Paved with Good Intentions: The American Experience and Iran*, Harmondsworth: Penguin Books 1981, p. 190.
8. N. R. Keddie, *Roots of Revolution*, Yale University Press 1981, p. 231.
9. Ramazani, *op. cit.* pp. 128, 139. Sullivan, the last US Ambassador to Iran, also mentions the Carter administration's contradictory position with respect to the Shah's regime. According to him, Carter had decided that the collaboration between SAVAK and the CIA should continue, while at the same time the US should attempt to persuade the Shah 'to improve the human-rights performance of his government in all its aspects'. W. H. Sullivan, *Mission to Iran*, New York and London: W. W. Norton 1981, pp. 20–22.
10. Keddie, *op. cit.* p. 231. One of the earliest voices of the opposition that surfaced was that of Haj Sayyed Javadi, a prominent essayist who initiated the series of open letters to the royal court with his two important letters of 1975 and 1976.
11. See E. Abrahamian, *op. cit.* p. 505; also E. Abrahamian, 'Iran: the political challenge', *MERIP Reports*, no. 69, July–August 1978, p. 4, where he reports that 5,000 students clashed with the police.
12. T. M. Ricks. 'The Iranian people under the Pahlavis: 1977–1978, years of demonstrations', *The Review of Iranian Political Economy and History*, vol. II no. 2, June 1978, p. 94.
13. *ibid.* p. 95.
14. *ibid.*
15. M. Fischer, *Iran from Religious Dispute to Revolution*, Harvard University Press 1980, p. 13.
16. See Keddie, *op. cit.* p. 242.
17. See the article entitled: 'Iran and the Black and Red Reactionaries', *Ettela'at*, 7 January 1978. Daryush Homayoun in his recent book writes that the article was written by the court and he merely acted as a messenger boy.
18. The regime gave the number of people killed as only two.
19. See Fischer, *op. cit.* pp. 194–95.
20. *The Review of Iranian Political Economy and History*, vol. II no. 2, 1978, p. 77.
21. According to *The Review of Iranian Political Economy and History*, vol. II no. 2, 1978, the police were forced to flee, see p. 77; according to Keddie *op. cit.* the police refused to get involved, see pp. 246–47.

22. See F. Halliday, *Iran: Dictatorship and Development*. Harmondsworth: Penguin Books 1979, p. 290.

23. *The Review of Iranian Political Economy and History*, vol. II no. 2, 1978, p. 78.

24. The government gave the number of dead as only six (see *Ettela'at*, 21 and 23 February 1978). European eye-witnesses stated about 100 (see Abrahamian, *op. cit.* p. 507; and Keddie, *op. cit.* p. 247). The opposition gave the number as 300 dead; and according to a source mentioned by *The Review of Iranian Political Economy and History*, Vol. II no. 2, 1978, p. 78, there were 500 killed.

25. Fischer, *op. cit.* p. 195.

26. See *ibid.* p. 196; Abrahamian, *op. cit.* p. 507 mentions about 100 killed in Yazd.

27. As many as 24 of these turned into riots and violent confrontations with the authorities, see Abrahamian, *op. cit.* p. 508.

28. SAVAK was assisted by a well-known civilian group of ultra-reactionary royalists, headed by Senator M. A. Massoudi, Buyuk Saber, P. Khosravani and a few other establishment figures, who organised mobs of mercenary thugs (known as *Chomagh-daran*) to attack demonstrations, meetings, and so on.

29. Abrahamian, *op. cit.* p. 508.

30. Nasiri was sent as ambassador to Pakistan; Moqadam was a lesser known figure among the general public.

31. See Abrahamian, *op. cit.* p. 511.

32. The slump in the construction industry was a major factor in the increase in unemployment: 'Private sector investment in construction increased only 7 per cent against 32 per cent in the previous year, starting a mini-recession', R. Graham, *Iran: The Illusion of Power*, London: Croom Helm 1979, p. 124; see also W. Branigan, 'Little joy greets Shah's anniversary', *Washington Post*, 20 August 1978, who mentions that there was a 30 per cent reduction in the wages of construction workers.

33. Eye-witness account from an American who was teaching at Pahlavi University in Shiraz, interviewed by *Middle East Research and Information Project Reports*, see text in nos. 75–76 April 1979, p. 14.

34. Abrahamian, *op. cit.* p. 513.

35. *Kayhan* newspaper, 30 August 1978, given in A. R. Nobari (ed.), *Iran Erupts*, Stanford: The Iran–America Documentation Group 1978, p. 183.

36. Keddie, *op. cit.* p. 250.

37. The reporter was Yves-Guy Berges, the following account is

based on his report published in *Le Figaro*, 9–10 September 1978, translated in Nobari, *op. cit.* pp. 197–201.
38. See Jean Gueyras, *Le Monde*, 11 September 1978.
39. See Abrahamian, *op. cit.* p. 516; also Nobari, *op. cit.* p. 196.
40. Gueyras, *op. cit.*
41. Jean Gueyras, *The Guardian*, 17 September 1978.
42. See *Middle East Research and Information Project Reports*, nos. 75–76, April 1979, p. 27.
43. 'How we paralysed the Shah's regime', *ibid.*
44. See 'The sun sets on the Peacock Throne', *Islamic Revolution*, vol. 1 no. 3, June 1979, p. 12.
45. Khomeini, reported in *The New York Times*, 1 November 1978.
46. See *The New York Times*, 6 November 1978.
47. See B. Rubin, *op. cit.* p. 224.
48. *Newsweek*, 20 November 1978.
49. Paul Balta, reporting from Abadan for *Le Monde*, see *Middle East Research and Information Project Reports*, nos. 75–76, April 1979, p. 18.
50. *ibid.* p. 18.
51. *Newsweek*, 20 November 1978.
52. M. R. Pahlavi, given in *ibid.*
53. See Fischer, *op. cit.* p. 204.
54. See Abrahamian, *op. cit.* p. 521.
55. Eye-witness account from Shiraz, *Middle East Research and Information Project Reports*, nos. 75–76, April 1979, p. 16.
56. Fischer, *op. cit.* p. 205.
57. T. Allway, 'Iran demonstrates', *Christian Science Monitor*, 12 December 1978.
58. *Financial Times*, 17 January 1978.

7. The overthrow of dictatorship

1. The estimated figure of 180,000 clergy, approximately one mulla for every 200 Iranians, is given in *Financial Times*, 12 December 1978; also by S. Zabih, *Iran's Revolutionary Upheaval: An Interpretive Essay*, San Francisco: Alchemy 1979, p. 20. For the breakdown of the numbers of clergy see E. Abrahamian, 'Structural causes of the Iranian revolution', *Middle East Research and Information Project Reports*, no. 87, May 1980, p. 24.
2. C. Goodey, 'Workers' Councils in Iranian factories', *Middle East Research and Information Project Reports*, no. 88, June 1980, pp. 6–7.

3. *ibid.* p. 8.
4. See B. Rubin, *Paved with Good Intentions: The American Experience and Iran*, Harmondsworth: Penguin Books 1981, pp. 245–46.
5. M. Fischer, *Iran from Religious Dispute to Revolution*, Harvard University Press 1980, p. 13.
6. See R. Apple, 'Shah's army is showing stresses', *New York Times*, 19 December 1978.
7. See R. Apple, 'A lull in the battle for Iran', *New York Times*, 3 February 1979.
8. See *Time*, 12 February 1979.
9. *Time*, 26 February 1979.
10. See *International Herald Tribune*, 11 February 1979.

8. The triumph of reaction

1. See Sharif Arani, 'Iran: from the Shah's dictatorship . . .', *Dissent*, no. 27, 1980, p. 13.
2. *The Economist*, 10–16 February 1979.
3. See C. Goodey, *Middle East Research and Information Project Reports*, June 1980, p. 7. This was according to the head of the committee, himself a former member of the factory administration under the old regime.
4. *ibid.* p. 6.
5. These included the committee of the tool factory in Tabriz, two or three factory committees in the northern province of Gilan (e.g. the lift-truck factory committee and the Union of Workers' Council of Gilan representing some 30,000 workers), and a few other committees in Tehran.
6. This organisation should not be confused with the radical Mojahedin guerrilla organisation.
7. For example, at Iran National Car Plant, General Motors, Leyland Motors, and of course within the oil industry. These committees were personally observed by A. Bayat and reported in his unpublished paper, 'Workers and workers' control in Iran', University of Kent, October 1982, p. 35.
8. See *Tehran Journal*, 22 February 1979.
9. The act, first passed in 1967, although it did not eliminate the *shari'a* (Islamic law) concerning such matters as marriage, did, however, modify it.
10. See E. Sanasarian, *The Women's Rights Movement in Iran*, New York: Praeger 1982, p. 125.
11. The ban on abortion was first introduced in September 1978 by the

government of Sharif-Emami as a concession to the militant clergy.

12. See the excellent article by Azar Tabari, 'The enigma of veiled Iranian women', *Middle East Research and Information Project Reports*, February 1982, pp. 22–27. See also N.R. Keddie, 'Iran: change in Islam; Islam and change', *International Journal of Middle East Studies*, vol. 11 no. 4, July 1980, p. 539; also 'Professional women on the wane', *The Iranian* (a journal published in Tehran) vol. 1 no. 3, 11 July 1979.

13. M. Poya, 'Murder, corruption, crisis', *Socialist Review*, November 1982, p. 9. This kind of 'temporary marriage' is perfectly legal under Islam and very common (it is called *sigheh*). See also *Women and Struggle in Iran*, a publication of the Women's Commission of the Iranian Student Association in the US, no. 1, March 1982, and no. 2, September 1982.

14. *The Guardian*, 13 March 1979.

15. Bazargan, a founding member and leader of the Iran Liberation Movement (a religious liberal organisation), was nominated by Khomeini on 5 February 1979 as provisional Prime Minister.

16. E. Rouleau, 'Khomeini's Iran', *Foreign Affairs*, vol. 59 no. 1, Fall 1980, p. 9.

17. *ibid.*

18. Although it was a common belief that within a matter of a few months many SAVAK agents had joined the *Komitehs* and local militias as bearded Islamic revolutionaries, it has also been suggested that many ex-officials of the Shah were killed off without public trial, so that they would not reveal the relations between some of the high clergy (e.g. Ayatollah Beheshti) and SAVAK.

19. See *The Economist*, 11 August 1979.

20. M. Ja'far and A. Tabari, 'Iran: Islam and the struggle for socialism', *Khamsin*, no. 8, 1981, p. 94.

21. Khomeini, quoted in *ibid.* pp. 94–95.

22. See *The Guardian*, 9 August 1979. Among other papers which failed to appear after August were, *Neday-e Azadi, Kayhan-e Azad, Paygham-e Emrouze* and *Ahangar*.

23. *The Guardian*, 14 August 1979.

9. Khomeini and the Islamic order

1. This is a mistranslation of *Velayat-e Faqih*, the 'Regency of the (Islamic) Jurist'.

2. On this see A. Sachedina, 'A treatise on the occultation of the

Twelfth Imamite Imam', *Studia Islamica*, vol. XLVIII, 1978,
pp. 109–24.

3. See Ruhullah al-Musavi Khomeini, *Kashf al-Asrar*, Persian edition
1979, p. 184.
4. See Khomeini, *The Islamic Government*, Najaf 1971 (in Persian) p. 32.
5. *ibid*. p. 53.
6. See Khomeini, *Kashf al-Asrar*, p. 185.
7. *ibid*.
8. Khomeini, *The Islamic Government*, p. 64.
9. See *The Guardian*, 28 June 1979.
10. Most of the measures implemented by Khomeini's regime were first
proposed by the Fadayian-e Islam in 1950. See 'Their programme:
the proclamation of Fadayian-e Islam' or 'The book of guidance
towards Truth', Tehran: 1329 (1950) (in Persian); the group is now
led by Khalkhali, the infamous 'hanging judge'.
11. *The Economist*, 10 February 1979.
12. Sharif Arani, 'Iran: from the Shah's dictatorship . . .', *Dissent*,
no. 27, 1980, pp. 12–13.
13. Khomeini's speech to Islamic students in Qom, given in B. Rubin,
Paved with Good Intentions: The American Experience and Iran,
Harmondsworth: Penguin Books 1981, p. 277.

10. Towards an Islamic theocracy

1. See *Ettela'at*, 19 August 1979.
2. Contrary to many suggestions among the exiled monarchical and
right-wing opposition, there is no evidence to substantiate their
claim that the regime itself instigated the US embassy occupation or
that Khomeini had personally ordered it.
3. 'The constitution of the Islamic Republic of Iran', English
translation (with an introductory note by R. K. Ramazani) in *The
Middle East Journal*, vol. 34 no. 2, Spring 1980, pp. 181–204. All
subsequent quotations are from this translation.
4. A French-educated economist son of a cleric, Bani-Sadr was an
active supporter of Mossadeq during the 1950s, joined the Islamic
Student Society while in exile in the 1960s and formulated an
'Islamic theory of economics'; became a member of the Islamic
Revolutionary Council and Khomeini's chief lay adviser and later
Foreign Minister, resigning during the hostage crisis.
5. Beheshti was one of the most powerful and influential figures of the
Islamic revolution, considered (after Ayatollah Taleghani's death)
as perhaps second only to Khomeini. It was, for example, Beheshti

who, as a member of the Islamic Revolutionary Council, headed a number of secret negotiations with General Huyser (Deputy Commander of US forces in Europe) during the final weeks of the Pahlavi dictatorship.
6. *The Guardian*, 9 June 1981.
7. However, a real threat (especially from the outside) to the Islamic republic may act as a catalyst in uniting, temporarily at least, the two tendencies.

11. The fight against reaction

1. Not that Bani-Sadr personally had any significant role in this transformation of the political climate. He had neither the base nor the political influence to organise armed resistance against the regime. But his fall signalled, especially for the Mojahedin, the end of any possibility of accommodation with Khomeini.
2. The IRP is in fact a very loose political party, made up of a coalition of a number of tendencies and factions. Beheshti, more than any other figure, held this coalition together and gave it an appearance of unity.
3. Quoted in *Iran Press Service*, no. 26, London: 24 June 1981.
4. See S. Zabih, *Iran Since the Revolution*, London: Croom Helm 1982, p. 205.
5. See *The Economist*, 26 September 1981.
6. See S. Zabih, *op. cit.* p. 205.
7. For example, Mossa Khiabani head of the Mojahedin's guerrilla operations in Iran.
8. See Manuchehr Hezarkhani's interview with Fred Halliday in *Middle East Research and Information Project Reports*, March/April 1982, p. 34.
9. *International Herald Tribune*, 4 January 1983.
10. *The Economist* gives a conservative figure of 12,000 executed (23 October 1982); the opposition estimates that at least 20,000 people have been executed between June 1981 to April 1982, see 'The organ of the Islamic Student Societies, followers of the Mojahedin', no. 63, 19 April 1982, p. 14.

12. Economic chaos: between crisis and collapse

1. See *Voice of Iran*, no. 3, October/November 1982, p. 6.
2. SAIPA car company, for example, laid off in 1979–80 about 40 per cent of its 2,500 workforce, see *Financial Times*, 8 January 1980.

3. *The Economist*, 17 July 1982.
4. See *Middle East Economic Digest*, vol. 26 no. 3, 15–21 January 1982. Precise figures on most economic activities are not available. The regime publishes few economic statistics, even though it is believed that the Central Bank of Iran still continues to collect data. However, there are some examples that indicate a decline in agricultural production. Wheat imports rose from 426,000 tons in 1978–79 to 2 million in 1980–81, see P. Clawson, 'Iran's economy: between crisis and collapse', *Middle East Research and Information Project Reports*, July–August 1981, p. 11. During the Rajai period it reached 2.4 million tons according to H. Keshavarz (a former agricultural planner, interviewed in Paris, October 1982). In 1981 the Islamic republic had bought $227.5 million worth of US farm products and a total of $1000 million-worth of food products from European countries, see *Middle East Economic Digest*, vol. 26 no. 3, 15–21 January 1982.
5. This proposal was known as *Band-e Jim*, or the 'J-paragraph' and was more of a political ploy than an agrarian policy; it was spearheaded by the IRP with the help of some left groups against the liberals.
6. According to S. Zabih, *Iran Since the Revolution*, London: Croom Helm 1982, p. 203, there are 4 million unemployed or 37 per cent; *Payam-e Daneshjoo*, no. 6, July 1982, gives the figure as 3–4 million; E. Rouleau ('Khomeini's Iran', *Foreign Affairs*, vol. 59 no. 1, 1980, p. 16) gives 2–4 million.
7. E. Rouleau, *op. cit.*
8. According to official sources 100,000 commercial licences were issued to street pedlars in 1979–80 in Tehran alone, see P. Clawson, *op. cit.* p. 15.
9. *ibid.* p. 13.
10. Japan has become an important market for Iranian oil, but this can hardly compensate for the drop in exports to other markets. In 1974, BP imported 2 million barrels per day from Iran – about 50 per cent of its total supplies. In 1980 it received only 125,000 barrels per day. The Japanese, however, kept their share of Iranian oil at the same level of 19–24 per cent, although it fell in absolute terms. See *Financial Times*, 4 January 1980 and *The Guardian*, 15 January 1980; see also V. Yorke, 'Oil, the Middle East and Japan's search for security', *International Affairs*, vol. 57 no. 3, Summer 1981, pp. 428–48.
11. Zabih, *op. cit.* p. 203, gives this figure of 85 per cent for 1981; *Payam-e Daneshjoo* gives 60–70 per cent; The Economist Society of

Iran quotes a consumer price increase of 50 per cent for 1980, see P. Clawson, *op. cit.* p. 12, as does Rouleau, *op. cit.* p. 16. Premier Moosavi stated in June 1982 that the annual rate of inflation was 14.5 per cent in May compared with 16.5 per cent in April, see *Middle East Economic Digest*, vol. 26 no. 28, 9–15 July 1982, p. 14.

12. See *Voice of Iran*, October–November 1982, p. 5.
13. See M. Poya, 'Murder, corruption, crisis', *Socialist Review* no. 48, November/December 1982, p. 10.
14. E. Rouleau, *op. cit.*
15. M. Poya, *op. cit.*
16. See P. Clawson, *op. cit.* p. 13.
17. In July 1982 there was a strike at the mill where 40,000 workers are employed (20,000 part-time), see M. Poya, *op. cit.* p. 11. Also, in April 1982, hundreds of workers at car assembly plants were arrested or dismissed following a series of strikes over the regime increasing the working week, see *Middle East Economic Digest*, vol. 26 no. 22, 28 May to 3 June 1982, p. 20.
18. It is believed that on average Iranian crude is sold at $28 per barrel, see *The Economist*, 11 September 1982; one source puts the figure as low as $26, see *The Guardian*, 8 September 1982. The official OPEC price at the time (1982) was $34 per barrel.
19. According to Iranian oil industry sources, production of oil went up to 2.2 million barrels per day in late May and early June 1982; however, average output for 1982 seems to have been slightly less than 2 million barrels per day; see *Middle East Economic Digest*, vol. 26 no. 25, 18–24 June 1982. About 400,000 barrels per day is for domestic (non-war) use, the rest for export, etc. Oil sales provided about 60 per cent of estimated state revenue of $31,866m in 1982, see *Middle East Economic Digest*, vol. 26 no. 6, 5–11 February 1982. In March 1983 oil output was officially put at 2.4 million barrels per day; unofficially the figure was put at 3 million a day. Income from oil sales for the year ended March 1983 was given as $23 billion.
20. The war with Iraq is obviously the most important reason for this depletion of assets.
21. See *Middle East Economic Digest*, vol. 26 no. 7, 12–18 February 1982, p. 18; *Foreign Report*, no. 1715, 11 February 1982, gives the figure of $650 million reserves for January 1982. However, according to diplomatic sources in Tehran, Iran's situation has improved considerably. Foreign currency reserves were put at $10 billion to $13 billion for the fiscal year 1983.

13. The struggle of national minorities

1. See *Tehran Journal*, 3 March 1979.
2. For example, Ayatollah Taleghani, Sheikh Ali Tehrani and Bani-Sadr.
3. *Le Monde*, 18 December 1979.
4. See 'The Organ of the European Organisation of KDP', Mehr 1361 (1982) p. 8, see also 'Kurdistan', the organ of the Central Committee of KDP.
5. The *Komala* and Ezzedin Husseini have refused to join the NCR, in part because of Bani-Sadr's role in the NCR. When Bani-Sadr was President he ordered the military offensive against the Kurds which resulted in the butchery of many Kurdish revolutionaries.
6. By July 1981, Baluchi guerrilla units (small in number) had become increasingly active against the Islamic authorities. However, there is, as yet, no Baluchi political organisation (at least in the Iranian section) that truly expresses the aspirations of the Baluchi people.
7. In this they were actively supported by the Fedayeen guerrillas who had not yet split into factions.
8. See *The Observer*, 8 May 1979. In an infamous incident Toomaj and three other members of the Fedayeen guerrillas were secretly murdered for their part in the Turkoman uprising.
9. Madani later became a presidential candidate (in 1980), receiving a large number of votes (perhaps as many as 2 million) many from the modern middle class, and soon after fled into exile. He is now one of many right-wing opposition leaders and should be remembered as the butcher of Arabs.
10. *The Guardian*, 6 July 1979.

14. The Iraq–Iran war

1. Khomeini's ambassador to Iraq, Doaey, has been implicated. Doaey joined Khomeini while he was in exile in Iraq and in a short time become relatively influential and a broadcaster on the Islamic opposition radio. This was established with the aid of the Ba'athist regime before it patched up its differences with the Shah in 1975 (the Algiers Pact).
2. See Eric Rouleau, 'The war and the struggle for the state', *Middle East Research and Information Project Reports*, July/August 1981, p. 4.
3. Quoted by C. Wright, 'Implications of the Iraq–Iran war', *Foreign Affairs*, vol. 59 no. 2, Winter 1980–81, p. 278.

4. See K. Kishtany, 'The Iraq–Iran war: the war of miscalculations', *Contemporary Review*, vol. 241 no. 1402, October 1982, p. 177; see also 'The secret Gulf pact', *Foreign Report*, no. 1649, 1 October 1980, p. 1.

5. Bakhtiyar and Oveissi paid four 'secret' visits to Baghdad between the end of August and mid-September 1980, 'The Gulf War', *Foreign Report*, no. 1648, 24 September 1980. In the last meeting of the conspirators on 18 September they were joined by General Palizban (a staunch royalist), who, according to some estimates, controls a force of some 2,000 former Imperial Army commandos. It has been suggested that the US intelligence services were also involved in the preparation of the invasion plan.

6. See Rouleau, *op. cit.*

7. Presumably General Palizban and his commandos would have a great deal to do with the Kurdish operation as they were rumoured to be the royalist counter-revolutionary force most active in that region.

8. *The Guardian*, 3 October 1980.

9. Reported by E. Rouleau, *The Guardian*, 21 October 1980.

10. See *The Guardian*, 16 October 1980.

11. K. Kishtany, *Contemporary Review*, 1982, p. 177.

12. According to the Iraqis there were some Iranian prisoners of war aged between 9 and 16, see *The Guardian*, 5 November 1982.

13. See the report by Robert Reid from Mandali (Iraq), *The Guardian*, 19 November 1982.

14. *The Economist*, 31 July 1982.

15. *The Guardian*, 4 October 1982.

16. *The Economist*, 2 October 1982.

17. Officially put at 1,870,000 by Asghar Samet, a spokesperson for the Interior Ministry, see S. Zabih, *Iran Since the Revolution*, London: Croom Helm 1982, note 19, pp. 194–95.

18. *ibid.* p. 195.

19. According to the International Solidarity Front for Defence of Democratic Rights in Iran (ISF-Iran) *News Bulletin*, no. 2, December 1982–January 1983, the current Iranian war budget is $14.2 billion, but according to the regime the war budget was $6.9 billion for 1982–83, see *The Guardian*, 14 October 1982. The cost of the war for Iraq is running at about $1 billion a month, see *The Economist*, 16 October 1982.

20. See E. Rouleau, *Middle East Research and Information Project Reports*, July/August 1981, p. 6.

21. See *Middle East Economic Digest*, vol. 26 no. 28, 9–15 July 1982.

22. Beginning in February 1979 with the execution or retirement of top officers and ending with a purge of some 10,000 men, many of whom were officers, mostly from the army, between September 1979 and September 1980, see W. F. Hickman, 'Ravaged and reborn: the Iranian army', Brookings Institution paper, 1982.
23. See *Middle East Economic Digest*, vol. 26 no. 31, 30 July–5 August 1982.
24. As a general rule those between the ages of 16 and 30, but this does not take into account the Basij recruitment of *much* younger boys.
25. In addition, any private company employing draft dodgers would have their firm shut for a period of six months for a first offence, and indefinitely after a second offence, see *Middle East Economic Digest*, vol. 26 no. 35, 27 August–2 September 1982.
26. *The Guardian*, 11 November 1982.
27. The relationship between the USSR and the Islamic republic has deteriorated sharply. One sign of this is the arrest of the members of the Central Committee of the Tudeh Party on charges of spying for Moscow in February 1983. However, the relations between the two countries is greatly influenced by the conflict between the Imam-line and the 'traditionalist-technocratic' tendencies, with the former in favour of closer relations and co-operation; the latter tendency includes factions totally opposed to any relations with the USSR or other communist countries.
28. See *Christian Science Monitor*, 6 August 1981.
29. See C. R. Denton, '"Tango November": the Israeli sale of US arms to Iran', *Middle East Perspective*, vol. XIV no. 6, October 1981, p. 3.

Chronology of political events in Iran, 1891–1982

1891–2	The Tobacco Protest. The bazaar strike and demonstrations on the streets, backed by the clergy, results in the annulment of the tobacco concession to a British company.
1901	Oil concession is granted by the Qajar Shah to William D'Arcy.
1905–6	The Constitutional Revolution. Iran becomes a constitutional monarchy.
June 1908	The civil war begins between the royalists and constitutionalists.
April 1909	Anglo-Persian Oil Company is formed.
July 1909	Royalists defeated by the constitutionalists.
1911	Russian and British troops enter northern and southern Iran.
1914–18	Iran is occupied by British, Russian and Turkish forces during First World War.
1917	The Jangali movement wins control of most of the northern Caspian province of Gilan.
May 1920	Soviet naval forces land a detachment of Red Army in the port of Enzeli in Gilan.
June 1920	Republic of Gilan is established and the Communist Party of Iran founded.
20 February 1921	Reza Khan's coup d'état.
25 April 1926	Reza Khan becomes Reza Shah Pahlavi and the monarchical military dictatorship is established.
August 1941	Reza Shah is forced to abdicate by the

	Allied occupation forces. His son, Mohammad Reza Pahlavi, is designated as the new Shah.
September 1941	The Tudeh ('Communist') Party is launched.
12 December 1945	The Democratic Party establishes a National Assembly in Azarbaijan.
22 January 1946	The first Kurdish Republic is proclaimed at Mahabad. Qazi Mohammad, is elected by the delegates of the Kurdish Democratic Party as president.
December 1946	The Iranian army enters Tabriz, capital of Azarbaijan, and also Mahabad, capital of the Kurdish Republic. The Kurdish and Azarbaijan nationalists are defeated.
February 1949	Assassination attempt on Shah. The Tudeh Party and the Central Council of the Federated Trade Unions of Iranian Workers and Toilers, are outlawed.
1949	A new political grouping, the National Front headed by Mohammad Mossadeq, appears as a dominant oppositional force.
1951	Mossadeq becomes Prime Minister. The oil industry is nationalised.
17 August 1953	Shah leaves Iran.
19 August 1953	A coup d'état instigated by the CIA and British Intelligence service topples Mossadeq.
1954	An oil consortium is formed by giant oil companies to take over from Anglo-Iranian Oil Company (renamed British Petroleum which now gains 40 per cent of Iranian operations).
1957	The National Information and Security Organization, SAVAK, is established.
1962	The 'first phase' of land reform programme begins. Local Council

	Election Bill: plan to enfranchise women.
January 1963	White Revolution.
May 1963	The theological school at Qom is attacked by security forces after student protests.
June 1963	Demonstrations against White Revolution. Khomeini is arrested; riots break out in Tehran, Qom and other major cities, resulting in many deaths.
1963	Two separate groups – later to merge and form the Fedayeen Guerrillas – split from the Tudeh Party and National Front to form clandestine organisations dedicated to armed struggle.
1965	The People's Mojahedin Organization is formed.
8 February 1971	The 'Siahkal incident': a small guerrilla group attacks the gendarmerie post in the village of Siahkal in the Caspian forest. Iran's guerrilla movement takes off.
March 1971	The People's Fedayeen Guerrilla Organization is formed.
August 1971	The Mojahedin begin their military operations.
March 1975	Shah dissolves the two-party system and creates the Resurgence Party.
May 1975	The Mojahedin split into two factions: the Islamic Mojahedin and a Maoist offshoot later known as the Paykar Organization.
June 1975	Demonstrations against the Resurgence Party marking the occasion of Khomeini's arrest in June 1963.
February 1977	Relaxation of police controls begin with the amnesty of 357 political prisoners.
May 1977	The protest of the intelligentsia surfaces

	in the form of open letters to the Court.
June–August 1977	Protest of 'city-limit' dwellers against 'slum clearance' programme; 50,000 demonstrate.
January 1978	Violent confrontation between 4,000 theology students and police in Qom, over a slandering article about Khomeini.
18 February 1978	Mass demonstration and riots in Tabriz.
29 March 1978	Violent political demonstrations spread to 55 urban centres.
June 1978	The first wave of strikes begins. The industrial working class enters the struggle against the dictatorship.
19 August 1978	The Abadan Tragedy. A cinema in the working-class district of Abadan is burnt with 410 men, women and children in it.
September 1978	Over half a million people march in Tehran demanding the end of the Pahlavis and the return of Khomeini.
7 September 1978	Martial law is declared in Tehran and 11 other cities.
8 September 1978	'Black Friday'. Hundreds of protestors murdered at a gathering in Jaleh Square, Tehran.
9 September 1978	Strike at Tehran oil refinery.
11 September 1978	Strike spreads to oil refineries of Isfahan, Abadan, Tabriz and Shiraz.
12 September 1978	Print workers' strike over martial law and censorship.
October 1978	Political strikes against the regime begin. Oil workers go on strike, reducing oil production from 5.8 million barrels per day to 1.1.
1 November 1978	The army is deployed in the oil fields.
6 November 1978	Shah appoints a military government headed by General Azhari.
11–12 November 1978	The army crackdown begins in the oil

	region, ending the oil strike.
December 1978	The religious month of Muharram brings millions of people onto the streets. Rooftop protests, chanting of 'Allah-o-Akbar', spreads to most urban centres.
4 December 1978	Oil workers strike again.
10–11 December 1978	Millions of people demonstrate under the banner of Islam. Soldiers in many towns joined the demonstrators.
30 December 1978	Bakhtiyar agrees to form a new 'reform' government.
31 December 1978	General Azhari resigns. A general strike brings the whole economy to a standstill.
16 January 1979	Shah leaves Iran. Jubilant crowds pour onto the streets of Tehran and other cities.
1 February 1979	Khomeini returns to Iran and is greeted by millions of people.
5 February 1979	Khomeini appoints Mehdi Bazargan as his provisional prime minister.
9 February 1979	The Imperial Guards attack the barracks of the mutinous airforce technicians in Tehran.
10–11 February 1979	The days of insurrection.
11 February 1979	The Pahlavi dictatorship is overthrown. Shah's Prime Minister, Bakhtiyar, escapes and armed youths take over the streets of most cities. Tehran Radio declares the Islamic Revolution's victory.
16 February 1979	50,000 military personnel demonstrate demanding a democratic army.
23 February 1979	Kurdish nationalists demonstrate demanding regional autonomy.
March 1979	Turkoman rebellion crushed by army and Islamic units.
8 March 1979	Women's demonstrations for equality and against the wearing of the veil.

April 1979	Iran becomes an Islamic Republic after a referendum.
August 1979	The crackdown against the left, Kurdish and other national and ethnic minorities begins.
3–4 August 1979	Election for the Assembly of Experts to examine the new Islamic constitution.
4 November 1979	US embassy is occupied. The hostage crisis begins and the Bazargan government resigns.
15 November 1979	The Assembly of Experts completes its work on the constitution.
2–3 December 1979	The Islamic constitution is ratified after a referendum. Violent confrontation between the supporters of Ayatollahs Shariatmadari and Khomeini takes place in Tabriz.
25 January 1980	Bani-Sadr is elected first president of the Islamic Republic.
April 1980	Khomeini begins his 'cultural revolution' to Islamicise all educational and cultural institutions. Islamic militants attack the left in their last sanctuaries, the universities.
18 April 1980	Bani-Sadr gives a 3-day ultimatum to all left-wing groups to evacuate their campus offices.
25 April 1980	An American rescue mission to free the hostages fails disastrously.
June 1980	A presidential decree makes the wearing of the veil compulsory in all government and public offices.
27 July 1980	The ex-Shah of Iran dies in exile in Egypt.
11 August 1980	Mohammed Ali Rajai becomes the Islamic Republic's new Prime Minister.
22 September 1980	Iran–Iraq war begins.
20 January 1981	American hostages are released as Reagan is being inaugurated.
March 1981	The conflict between Bani-Sadr and the

	Islamic Republican Party turns violent after a rally sponsored by Bani-Sadr is attacked.
June 1981	Bani-Sadr is dismissed as Commander-in-Chief, and is forced to go into hiding.
20 June 1981	Country-wide urban guerrilla warfare begins against Khomeini's regime.
28 June 1981	An explosion kills 72 of the top leadership of the Islamic Republican Party.
July 1981	Bani-Sadr and Masud Rajavi (the leader of the Mojahedin) escape to France.
30 August 1981	A second explosion kills the newly appointed President Rajai and his Prime Minister, Bahonar.
September 1981	Liquidation of all opposition elements in factories and other workplaces begins.
March 1982	Iranian offensive against Iraq changes the war in favour of Iran.
11 April 1982	President Saddam Hussein of Iraq declares that the main aim of Iraq is now to prevent an Iranian invasion of Iraqi territory.
7 November 1982	Iranian forces penetrate 4 to 7 miles into Iraq.